HARLAXTON COLLEGE

D1352173

362.29/Jos

HARLAXTON MANOR
GRANTHAM LINE

Agenda *Speed*

THIS IS A CARLTON BOOK

Design copyright © 2000 Carlton Books Limited
Text copyright © 2000 Carlton Books Limited
Pictures © various, see Picture Acknowledgements

This edition published by Carlton Books Limited 2000
20 Mortimer Street
London
W1N 7RD

This book is sold subject to the condition that it shall not, by
way of trade or otherwise, be lent, resold, hired out or otherwise
circulated without the publisher's prior written consent in any
form of cover or binding other than that in which it is published
and without a similar condition including this condition, being
imposed upon the subsequent purchaser.

All rights reserved.

A CIP catalogue for this book is available from the British Library.

ISBN 1 85868 861 2

Design: Adam Wright/bluefrog
Picture research: Prudence Korda
Production: Garry Lewis

Agenda

Speed

Miriam Joseph

UNIVERSITY OF EVANSVILLE
HARLAXTON COLLEGE LIBRARY
HARLAXTON MANOR
GRANTHAM, LINCS

CONTENTS

ACKNOWLEDGEMENTS

The author wishes to thank the Independent Study for Drug Dependence and Sona Mahtani for all their help during the writing of this book. The author also wishes to thank Channel 4 and Duncan at Windfall Films, who gave permission for copyrighted material from the TV series 'Rush' to be reproduced.

PICTURE ACKNOWLEDGEMENTS

The publishers would like to thank the following sources for their kind permission to reproduce the pictures in this book:

Corbis/Bettmann 32

Hulton Getty 21, 25, 28, 44, 51, 64, 66/7

The Image Bank/Archive Photos 6, 19, 39, 47, 56 reuse, 82/David de Cossy 17/Nino Mascardi 9/Kaz Mori 70/D. Redfearn 58

Photofusion/Mark Campbell 11, 94 reuse

Tony Stone Images/Bruce Ayres10/Coney Jay 15/D Young Riess 74

Every effort has been made to acknowledge correctly and contact the source and/or copyright holder of each picture, and Carlton Books Limited apologises for any unintentional errors or omissions which will be corrected in future editions of this book.

INTRODUCTION

Illicit drugs are one of the biggest leisure activities in the world today, representing an estimated US$400 billion per annum industry. During the twentieth century they moved, despite the best efforts of governments and law enforcers, from the underground into the mainstream. This series of books tells the stories of these drugs, from their initial synthesis and use as therapeutic or medical aids, to their adoption as adjutants to pleasure. It also tells of the increasingly draconian legislation attendant as each drug moved from the medical to the sybaritic world.

Speed was doled out like sweeties for all manner of ailments during the twentieth century, but mainly for tiredness and as an appetite suppressant. But soon the spectacle of a million housewives ironing at the speed of light became too much for the authorities to bear and speed joined other once reputable drugs in the dustbin of illegality. Taken up instead by generation after generation of teenagers, speed became the drug par excellence of the youth movement.

THE SPEED EFFECT

Speed is a stimulant drug that gives the impression of amplifying the body's mental and physical resources. After taking speed, energy levels soar, confidence screams out and the capacity for intense concentration seems to be greatly enhanced. "Speed" is actually the street name for an entire family of chemically related synthetic stimulants called amphetamines. The amphetamine family is divided into the following three pharmaceutical classes – the most common brand names are shown in brackets: leavoamphetamine (Benzedrine), dexamphetamine (Dexedrine) and methamphetamine (Methedrine). All three drugs differ greatly in potency but essentially produce similar behavioural and physiological effects. Laevoamphetamine is the weakest, dexamphetamine is twice as strong and methamphetamine is twice as strong again.

Strictly speaking, "amphetamines", the plural form of the word, only applies to these three drugs, although in its broadest context the term can embrace a large number of related substances. Unlike some street drugs, amphetamines do not occur in nature and so can only be made in a chemical laboratory. "Speed" is the most commonly used and understood non-scientific term for all amphetamine-related synthetic stimulants.

When any kind of amphetamine enters the body, it rushes to the central nervous system (CNS), heightening brain and spinal cord activity. This enhances levels of arousal and results in greater awareness and a heightened ability to respond to the world around us. Speed is essentially the great pretender, a charlatan that deceives the body into adjusting to heady heights of nervous activity by naturally altering its internal thermostat. This is because the chemical structure of the amphetamine family closely resembles that of a naturally occurring chemical nerve-impulse transmitter called noradrenaline (norepinephrine in the USA). As a result, speed acts on the CNS in much the same way that noradrenaline does. An influx of speed into the bloodstream is interpreted by the CNS as an increase of noradrenaline and so the nervous system makes the necessary adjustments to power up the body proportionately. The more noradrenaline the nervous system perceives, the faster and harder the body is cranked up to respond.

THE GREAT PRETENDER

Yet speed in itself does not provide the apparent increase in energy that is experienced. This energy must be drawn from the body's own finite stocks. Like an insidious thief in the night, speed forces open the body's energy reserves, allowing almost instant access. As speed does not add to the body's energy resources, the user will feel tired after the effects have worn off and it can take a couple of days for the body to return to normal. The impact on the body from a speed excursion is exhaustion and depression. A temporary chemical crash of this sort is inevitable – there is no "free lunch" to be had. As time progresses, the initial euphoria and self confidence gives way to a psychosis marked by abrupt mood changes, possible aggressive behaviour, paranoid delusions and hallucinations of sight, sound, touch and smell. The user may actually believe these hallucinations to be real.

METHODS OF USE

There are four main ways in which speed is used: swallowing, smoking, "snorting" (sniffing) and by injection.

Swallowing: The traditional way to take speed has been to swallow the drug in pill form. Pharmaceutically produced speed pills that find their way on to the street are commonly referred to as "bennies", "dexxies" and "uppers". A method that has become popular in recent years is to roll up a dose of amphetamine sulphate inside a cigarette paper and swallow it, perhaps chased by a drink. This is known as a "bomber".

Smoking: The smokeable, super-charged version of regular cocaine is called "crack". The equivalent, as far as amphetamine is concerned, is called "ice". Whereas crack is simply cocaine in its chemical base form, ice is chemically identical to methamphetamine; it has

SPEED PILLS

simply been concocted in a different physical form, having been allowed to "crystallize" during production. It is much more concentrated than basic amphetamine sulphate and has the appearance of a dense, sparkly rock. The ice crystal is usually heated in an incense burner or in a glass pipe. The resulting vapours are inhaled. One of the peculiar properties of ice is that, after being smoked, a small part remains in the pipe, returning to its solid state. This residue can then be reheated and the vapours once more inhaled – a ritual that can be repeated three or four times, although with diminishing results.

Snorting: The snorting method involves chopping up the crystalline powder form of the drug so that it is fine enough not to scrape the inside of the nostrils. The chopping is done on a mirror or any hard flat surface using a razor blade. A thin line, 5–8cm (2–3in) long is formed and this is drawn up through the nose using a rolled up bank note, a ball-point pen case or – for those who don't care for ceremony – without any tools whatsoever. Sniffed speed takes effect within about twenty minutes and the more intense effects last from four to six hours in the body.

Injecting: Crude amphetamine sulphate can be injected by dissolving it in water and filtering it through a clean cigarette tip to remove the chalk, but it is the more potent methamphetamine that is prized among the injecting cognoscenti. This is principally because of the exhilarating "rush" that the drug provides at the moment that it

SNORTING SPEED

SPEED CAN MAKE YOU DANCE TILL YOU DROP

is injected. Users claim the hit is like no other and compare it with a whole body orgasm. The rush occurs immediately the liquid is injected and has disappeared within half a minute. In the US, methamphetamine has developed something of a cult following. But since the late 1960s, stocks have been difficult for users in the UK to come by.

THE PARTY DRUG

Like all stimulant drugs, in the short term amphetamines produce feelings of exhilaration, increased energy, a sense of well-being, power and confidence, an enhanced ability to concentrate and a marked reduction in the need for sleep and food. Thus speed has found favour as a "functional" drug with many groups of workers and as a "recreational" drug, among those who want to stay up and dance the night away. In moderate doses, speed causes wakefulness and euphoria, increases motor activity and performance and suppresses appetite, thereby reducing food and water intake. As an appetite suppressant, the drug's potential for aiding weight loss has made it particularly popular with women.

Speed tends to intensify the users' feelings and emotions about themselves and the world around them. Low to moderate doses do not disrupt thought patterns, individuals speak quite rationally, but can be very talkative and sometimes a bit aggressive. What, to the user, might seem to be brilliant flashes of insight, succinctly and forcefully expressed, may appear to others to be nonsensical rubbish.

At higher doses, the CNS can become over-stimulated, resulting in insomnia, restlessness, nervousness, paranoia, anxiety, irritability and aggression. Blood pressure and pulse rate are generally, but not always, increased due to the stimulation of the nervous system. Even when the initial effects are pleasant, they are often followed by depression and fatigue. Sustained use of speed leads to increased tolerance to the substance and hence the need to increase the intake in order to get the same "high" or sense of euphoria that was felt before.

Irritability, suspiciousness, heightened aggression and an unpleasant "wired" sensation may be strongly experienced. To relieve these symptoms, some users turn to alcohol, sedatives or opiates. Rapid changes in mood, flights of ideas, and a self-evident physical tension and restlessness are warning signs to any companions or bystanders that impulsive violence could occur at any time. As the drug wears off, the user is likely to feel depressed and washed out.

Binges are followed by a short period of exhaustion and sleep, from which the user emerges into a phase of lethargy and inertia, often accompanied by anxiety or depression which can become intense enough to induce thoughts of suicide or self-harm. The temptation to use more speed is tremendous at this stage but, if it is successfully resisted, the mood can be expected to gradually return to normal. Occasionally, anxiety or depression has been known to persist for months or even years.

Even among those who use only small amounts of the drug, a marked psychological dependence can occur in response to the sense of well-being that is brought on by speed and there is a very high rate of relapse among regular users who try to stop.

LONG-TERM PROBLEMS

Heavy speed use puts a strain on the cardiovascular system leading to high blood pressure, irregular heart rhythm and possible stroke, if the drug is not discontinued, and injury to the small blood vessels serving the eye can lead to retinal damage. Speed also often seems to cause a rash, and heavy users may find that their teeth rot because of the loss of dentine. Frequent use causes a rapidly diminishing sensitivity to the euphoric effects but not to the potentially dangerous effects on the heart – yet reported deaths due to the overdose of speed are rare.

Those who are malnourished as a result of prolonged speed use may suffer calcium deficiency and anorexia and women may stop menstruating and become temporarily infertile. Speed taken in pregnancy can pose a risk to the healthy development of the baby's heart and bile system and has been linked with cleft palate. It is also said to be associated with underweight babies. Reliable information is hard to come by in this area, however, and the full extent of these effects is unknown.

SENSORY OVERLOAD

The stereotypical view of powerful stimulants such as speed and cocaine is that they hype people up into a very aggressive state. They put the nervous system into overdrive, inducing a kind of sensory overload and leading to irritability, paranoia and loss of judgement. While none of this is untrue – in practice it is a little more complex than that. Speed can actually give hitherto wound-up, insecure people the chemical elevation they need to help them relax. This also works with aggressive adults as well as with some children who have been diagnosed as hyperactive/hyperkinetic. Alcohol (a CNS depressant) operates in much the same way. Some people who drink want to start fights, whereas others become uncharacteristically smoochy and lovey-dovey.

What happens then when alcohol and speed are mixed? Again reports vary. One person reported that speed completely obliterated any effect that alcohol had had on him. Another user said that she felt OK if she drank alcohol and then took speed, but if she took speed first and then drank she would get into a foul-mouthed fighting frenzy, with no recollection the next day of what she had done. The Manchester drug agency, Lifeline, warns that combining alcohol and a couple of grams of speed can assist a person who would normally have crashed out on a skinful of booze to *"stay awake long enough and retain enough energy to act on their drunken impulses. This is worrying from the point of view of both HIV prevention and public order and safety."*

AMPHETAMINE PSYCHOSIS

Some individuals who use speed can go into what the professionals call an "amphetamine psychosis", so named because in most respects it is comparable to the symptoms experienced by schizophrenics. On the streets, this condition is more graphically described by speed users as the "horrors"! In both cases there are vivid auditory hallucinations as well as paranoid delusions. The drug-induced psychosis might start with a vague and not unpleasant curiosity; a desire to look beneath the surface of things. Other people and their actions become entrancing and are scrutinized. But those other people then appear to be scrutinizing the speed user; watching and following. Noises, colours, and other stimuli are sharply experienced, which can invoke hallucinations. Some people lapse into obsessional behaviour – ironing and scrubbing through the night, or pointlessly dismantling and reassembling gadgetry such as radios and car engine parts.

THE McGYVER EFFECT

Prolonged speed use can result in periods filled with paradoxical patterns of activity. People typically spend a lot of their time "tweaking" – a term used about someone who is fixated for hours on the same activity of "fixing", "tinkering" or even "artistic crafting". This habit of constantly taking things apart and putting them back together was so common in California at one time that people began to call it the "McGyver Effect", after a popular television show in which the hero, a cash-strapped sleuth, created ingenious contraptions out of assorted material in order to catch criminals. In the case of speed users, however, the effect worked the other way round – a useful appliance often ended up unintentionally as an ingenious collection of assorted parts.

For many speed users, "tweaking" gives them a licence to tinker, to perform with some kind of goal, but always free of deadlines. Many users have complained that they have a lot of energy but never manage to finish any job properly. One user explained it like this:

"Speed was making me fast, but I was going nowhere, I couldn't finish anything. I'd start a little of this, go to that, I'm moving real fast, but I was getting nothing done." So, being busy while high on speed had a paradoxical effect, or as someone else described it, *"...speed is a really funny name for this drug! The longer you do it, the slower you get! ...It's like watching the wheels of a car spinning so fast it starts to turn backward or even stand still. That's what speed does."*

Pointless, repetitive behaviour sometimes appears, and there may be involuntary picking and scratching at the skin, as if trying to remove imaginary bugs – "meth bugs" as they are known. These symptoms usually disappear slowly after a week or so of abstinence, but occasionally they can last much longer or become indistinguishable from schizophrenia.

An arresting account of speed paranoia appeared in the *Journal of Drug Issues*, as relayed by a San Francisco male sex worker:

"You're walking down the street, or you're on a bus and you're kind of looking around and you automatically think everyone knows you are on this drug. Then you hear someone clapping their hands and you think they are motioning toward you and they may be two or three blocks away.... You may see things like someone standing on the corner and you think they are following you or watching you....

You think, so I've been walking up and down the street so many times and everyone is bound to know me now and so you're walking down the street and you see the bus go by and you know you may not be dressed for the day and everybody in the bus looks at you and the bus driver honks the horn at somebody in the street and you don't know this and you think it's all directed toward you."

The major difference between traditional psychosis and one that is speed-induced is that the drug user's symptoms will invariably vanish once the body is free of the drug – usually within a few days, and rarely after more than a week. Also, in amphetamine psychosis, consciousness and memory generally stay clear and there is a keen appreciation of time, place and identity. Such fundamentals become quite murky and unclear in people who are classed as schizophrenic.

The onset of amphetamine psychosis is frequently related to heavy, long-term speed use. However, new users with a predisposition to addiction are also very vulnerable. Another serious problem is that speed use can trigger authentic schizophrenia in those people who have an undiagnosed inherited tendency toward the condition.

DEPENDENCE AND ADDICTION

Just as the lure of heroin for those who dabble in it has been over-dramatized, so the pulling power of speed has been consistently underestimated and understated. As with heroin, the attraction is a combination of the physical and the psychological, with the user becoming more dependent on the release of energy and confidence while feeling more and more uncomfortable during the correspondingly low periods between use. This can change into an escalating pattern of dangerous use.

After withdrawal from the drug, the effect can be precisely the reverse of whatever the drug was offering; instead of euphoria and the curbing of appetite and sleep, there will be excessive hunger and fatigue. With speed, there is no real physical withdrawal syndrome comparable to that experienced by heroin users. The user will

AMPHETAMINE PSYCHOSIS – THE DOWN SIDE

not feel physically ill with cramps, fever, sweating and so on as a result of stopping the use of speed. However, the feelings of extreme fatigue, hunger, depression and a disturbance of sleep following a bout of prolonged use constitutes a pattern of withdrawal effects, particularly as these feelings disappear with the resumption of speed use. While this is of a different nature from heroin withdrawal, there is no doubt that speed withdrawal can be equally or sometimes more distressing.

Tolerance to speed causes many regular, long-term users to build the doseage up to several grams of street speed every day. See-sawing moods, poor concentration, insomnia, fluctuating periods of suspiciousness and paranoia are quite common. There may be heavy consumption of alcohol, tranquillizers or opiates in an attempt to overcome these effects. Painful physical symptoms are not very common in those who stop taking speed but depression, fatigue, lack of pleasure in life, extreme craving for drugs and sleep disturbances are common and may last for weeks or months.

Some community surveys have been carried out that indicate that the majority of speed consumers use the drug quite infrequently, in relatively modest doses taken orally. In these circumstances, the likelihood of serious problems seems quite low. Adverse effects correlate quite closely with dose and frequency of use, and are much more common in those who inject speed. The likelihood of drug-related problems is unsurprisingly greater in those with pre-existing mental health problems, and inversely related to educational attainment.

THE SPEED RUN

If the drug is injected, the physiological and psychological effects are heightened. With injection, users will feel a sudden intense sensation or "rush". This rush is sought after with every consequent hit of the drug. Regular users of both oral and injectable speed may embark on a session of extended speed use or a "run". The phenomenon of the speed run is well known in drug circles. It lasts up to several days and is an attempt, by repeated injections, to hang on to the initial feelings of exhilaration and mastery, often neglecting food and sleep. By the second day there is no more rush and the high feelings are replaced by agitation in the body and spirit. Typically, these sensations intensify over the next three to five days, during which time the user probably won't eat or sleep and will usually inject more speed, more often.

The run ends when either the supply or the user is spent. Sleep will follow – usually for forty-eight hours or more. Upon waking there will be feelings of grogginess, depression, dehydration and hunger – the last two because of the drug's appetite-suppressing qualities. With long-term use of speed, users rapidly develop a tolerance –

particularly if the user is injecting the drug. Users on speed runs may build up to doses of two grams or more in a vain attempt to recapture that initial "rush".

The features of speed overdosing include muscle spasms, racing pulse and a high temperature. However, in the UK, although the drug has been a constant on the dance scene as it has evolved since the 1960s, there have been no recorded deaths resulting from over-heating (unlike Ecstacy) or overdosing. Deaths are usually associated with injecting, either as a direct overdose or complications arising out of the intravenous use of the drug.

The needle doesn't appeal to most speed snorters, even heavy users of the drug. But as speed has largely escaped the stigma surrounding heroin junkies, the excess use of speed – even via a needle – has yet to be flagged up as a major problem. Not only is speed far more popular than heroin, several surveys have shown that those who inject it tend to be younger and more sexually active than intravenous opiate users. They probably share their needles more, as they're less likely to have dealings with drug agencies that offer free replacements at needle exchanges, and they are more likely to have sex without a condom and with a variety of partners.

While there can be few functioning adults left in the Western world who remain unaware of the basic message in relation to HIV and AIDS, there is much less known about the equivalent risk of catching and passing on tuberculosis or the hepatitis strains B and C. The trouble with speed is that it tends to encourage feelings of omnipotence: *I am all-powerful, nothing can hurt me.*

Added to this is another consideration: while speed injectors might appreciate the risks, they might be too embarrassed to say no to an unwashed barrel of speed when it is passed their way – perhaps from a friend. Or they might feel unable, during the heat of foreplay, to ask their sexual partner to put on a condom.

Disease risks aside, intravenous users of speed should take care to grind up their powder or pills as fine as possible. This is to avoid any insoluble particles getting stuck in the small blood vessels of the lungs and the brain. Abscesses are

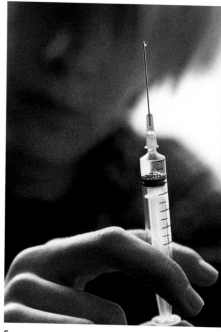

SHOOTING UP

common among injectors, as is inflammation of the walls of the veins, and infections in or around the entry site of the needle. Any of these afflictions can be caused by adulteration in the street product, inept injection techniques, the use of unsterilized needles, or by repeated injection into the same site.

The purity of street speed can sometimes be as low as one per cent. But there is always the chance that a much stronger batch of speed could turn up and, if injectors are not forewarned so they can dilute the drug, it could put a serious strain on the heart and brain. Here is an anecdote that serves as a salutary lesson that things are not always as they seem. Sometime in 1976, researchers at the University of Chicago injected two groups of cocaine users – one with 16mg of cocaine, the other with 10mg of speed. Initially, the groups were hard pressed to tell any difference between the two hits. It only became obvious when the coke rush faded after twenty minutes. Those injected with speed were still feeling the high well over an hour later.

Users who find the duration of these effects hard to believe should bear in mind that the normal level of purity in a gram of illicitly-produced amphetamine sulphate is around five percent, and the normal level of purity in the more potent methamphetamine hydrochloride is at around sixty percent. Consequently, it is quite easy to understand and recognize the really very powerful punch that the amphetamine family packs.

DRUG SPEAK

Culturally speaking, one of the more fascinating things about illicit drug use has been the evolution of drug jargon that is specific to a country. Different parts of the world have adopted their own names for the various drugs. As a result, each drug can have at least twenty different nicknames or street names. Cannabis, the most widely used illicit drug in the world, has in excess of two hundred different street names the world over!

Because of the demonization and criminalization of drugs and drug users, those involved with drugs have developed an alternative idiom in which to communicate about their product, so as not to arouse suspicion. There has developed a kind of drug-speak around every facet of drug use – from the manufacturing to the dealing, procuring and use of drugs. From picking up the "gear" or the "stash" and then finding a place to get a "fix", a "hit" or a "toke", hoping it will lead to the "rush" or the "kick" or the "blast" and then inevitably resulting in the "comedown" or the "crash", every possible step in the process of using drugs has developed a corresponding street vernacular.

IN THE BEGINNING...

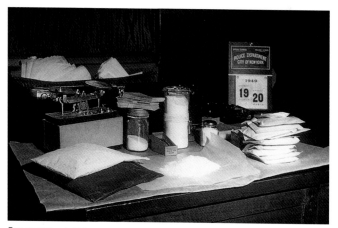

Early days – a cache of drugs

Speed might have been born in a laboratory, but the chemical make-up of this manufactured drug bears a great many similarities to a naturally-occurring compound found in a plant called *Ephedra vulgaris*. The use of this herb as a stimulant is thought to have an ancient history, dating back at least fifty thousand years, and so is considered to be the earliest known plant valued for its psychoactive properties. Pollen remains of six plants, including ephedra, were found in a Neanderthal grave at a place called Shanidar, in Iraq. Subsequent research into this discovery encouraged the leading archaeologist, Solecki, to propose that these plants had medicinal uses in Neanderthal society and were not just picked for ornamental purposes. Solecki's ideas were given more weight when, at a dig in prehistoric temples in Central Asia, archaeologists found the remains of ephedra in contexts that related it to both cannabis and opium. This find suggests that ephedra could have been an important ingredient in psychoactive preparations of the time.

Since early times, the Chinese have used species of ephedra to combat coughs and lung complaints. In 1887, a Japanese pharmacologist named Dr Nagayoshi Nagai isolated the ephedra plant's active ingredient, ephedrine. Dr Nagai went on to synthesize methamphetamine from ephedrine in 1893. But this discovery lay dormant, just like amphetamine itself, and failed to attract much attention as a pharmaceutical product until well into the next century. Ephedrine's importance as a stimulant was not realized in Europe until the late 1920s, and it was only in the 1930s that ephedrine began to be used in the effective treatment of asthma patients.

SPEED THERAPY

Amphetamine was first synthesized by the scientist Edeleano in a chemical laboratory in Germany in 1887 – the same year that ephedrine was isolated. But it was not until many years later, in 1927, that the therapeutic potential of the amphetamine family was realized, when it was discovered that these drugs – as well as raising blood pressure and constricting the blood vessels – opened up the small bronchial sacs in the lungs, allowing easier breathing. Gordon Alles, a chemist working in Los Angeles, recognized that amphetamine would be a cheap substitute for ephedrine in the treatment of asthma. As ephedrine was extracted from a herb found in China, there were fears in the medical and pharmaceutical establishments that supplies would soon become exhausted. The discovery of a cheap synthetic drug, with a known and controllable composition, that was not vulnerable to the variable quality and availability of a natural herb from a far-away foreign land, was a major step forward. It was Alles' work that initially identified some of the medicinal uses to which amphetamine could be put.

Amphetamine was soon being prescribed by medical practitioners for depression and also for the treatment of other hitherto incurable conditions, such as narcolepsy, a disorder involving sudden severe attacks of sleepiness throughout the day. Its usefulness seemed endless: soon it began to appear as a medicinal product prescribed for a long list of illnesses, including Parkinson's disease and epilepsy. One side effect of speed is that it suppresses the appetite and so it was prescribed for the control of obesity. Scientists built careers on the seemingly limitless uses of speed.

In early 1932, speed was introduced as a nasal decongestant by the pharmaceutical company, Smith, Kline and French (SKF), after F. P. Nabenhauer, their chief chemist, developed Benzedrine in an inhaler

"I'VE GOT JUST THE THING" SAID THE DOCTOR

form that could be sold over the counter. The company became giants in the bronchial dilator business and soon marketed amphetamine sulphate as Benzedrine inhalers and tablets, suitable for asthmatics and those suffering from hay fever and colds. The marketing of this substance soon began in earnest, especially in the form of oral preparations for ease of use. Speed was first launched in the USA, UK and Germany and then in other countries.

THE HARD SELL

Once the pharmaceutical world cottoned on to what it saw as the therapeutic value of speed it went into overdrive. Speed was heralded as an alleviator of many of the illnesses that beset the rich and working poor alike – a gift to the world, able to help people cope with the numerous everyday problems that affect the typical family. It was promoted as being completely safe and effective without any risks, especially not that of addiction. Many papers in the reputable medical literature of the day reported very favourable results and fuelled this enthusiasm. Only in hindsight can the poor scientific quality of most of this work be seen. The subsequent loss of innocence regarding the use of speed has since been blamed on deviant elements in society getting their hands on this drug. The truth is that speed was introduced to society as a "wonder drug" with no harmful side effects. But once ordinary people took this information at face value and began to use the drug on a regular basis, they came to be demonized.

Speed took off as *the* drug and the first port of call for many physicians. It was recommended for an ever-widening range of conditions including asthma, epilepsy, obesity, travel sickness, narcolepsy, schizophrenia, impotence, Parkinson's disease, hyperactive disorders in children and apathy in old age (for which it seemed quite convincingly effective). "Speeding" the elderly and infirm in this manner would have a touch of ironic humour today, if it were not completely at odds with the innocence and naiveté that seemed to surround the drug in those early days. A 1946 report listed thirty-nine different disorders for which Benzedrine – only one of the three main kinds of amphetamine – was the recommended treatment.

What was happening socially and economically also shaped the growth of speed, which held a unique place in the pharmaceutical marketplace. Economic depression in the 1930s made speed a very attractive and legitimate coping mechanism to have in the medicine cupboard. In the absence of other effective pharmaceutical remedies for depression, doctors were relieved to be able to offer speed to their patients. The Second World War also contributed to its acceptance as a valuable and legally endorsed drug when many troops were supplied with speed to delay fatigue, boost morale and enhance alertness. Ironically, it was this capacity to provide unabated energy and confidence that went on to ensure the cult status of speed as a good-time drug on the street scene.

In the USA in the 1940s, there was little need for an illicit market in speed. Legally manufactured pharmaceutical tablets could be bought wholesale over the counter by any adult at a price of about fourteen pills per penny – a staggering 75 cents per thousand speed pills. It would not be hyperbole to say that speed was being sold like sweets are sold to kids. Tablets continued to be available over the counter without prescription until 1951. During the 1950s and 1960s, amphetamines were being widely prescribed for fatigue, as slimming aids and even marketed in combination with barbiturates as Drinamyl ("purple hearts") for depression. In 1958, 3.5 billion tablets were produced in the USA alone – enough to supply every man, woman and child in the country with twenty standard doses. Not only people with medical conditions were using them, but also those with everyday problems and concerns. The popularity of these pills was bolstered by their low cost and long-lasting effect. Speed almost became commonplace, as was reflected in its use by all sorts of people, including students, businessmen, truck drivers and housewives.

The post-war era and the early 1950s was a period of rapid social change and this encouraged the take-up of speed in society. There was increased urbanization, improved technology and the emergence of a specific youth or teen culture. Greater access to television meant people were now bombarded with images of idealized lifestyles, creating much higher expectations about the way their own lives should be shaping up. Household gadgets, cars and all manner of technological innovations meant that the public – and especially the young – had many more options open to them and much more time on their hands in which to explore them. All of these factors contributed to the faster pace of society. The pace of people's lives was getting faster too – and speed seemed the perfect companion.

Speed's energy enhancing qualities had a powerful impact. Advertising slogans reflected the mood of the day: "Re-energize for life in the fast lane", "Come alive", "Feel good" were all slogans used to sell speed – and sell they certainly did. Sales campaigns featured advertisements such as "Two pills are better than one month's vacation", and soon there were moderate and immoderate users all over the world. Advertising for miracle speed cures for weight problems also caught the public imagination. Dieting was becoming increasingly popular and there was a seemingly insatiable appetite for dietary aids. Speed-based diet aids were sold with no regulation at all. There were even "cash for pounds off" deals. Women were enticed not only with images of perfect bodies but also with cash prizes. *"Katherine Carson of Texas received $5,000 for losing 126lbs in just four months and she's just one of thousands of satisfied customers of our CASH and ACHIEVEMENT award program."*

The casual use of speed became commonplace – especially by military personnel on night operations, factory workers or hospital staff on night shifts, truck drivers on extended duties and students preparing for examinations. By today's standards, such casual consumption – and even most of the therapeutic uses to which the drug was being put – would be regarded as "misuse" or "abuse" of speed. In those early days, however, there were no clear indicators as to what might constitute speed abuse. It was mainly speed's integration into "street" culture that brought about its redefinition as a dangerous drug.

The popularity of speed seemed to drive its production and, in turn, higher production levels served ultimately to drive up the popularity of speed. Legal production in the USA soared from 3.5 billion tablets in 1958 to 10 billion tablets by 1970. Speed was a profitable business and there were vested interests who were happy to keep things that way. Meanwhile, continuing medical research remained unscrutinized by the public and unpublicized by the manufacturing establishment. Records show that by the 1950s the pharmaceutical companies were perfectly well aware that speed had addictive properties but they didn't sound a single note of caution. The drive for profits initially overrode any questions and concerns and business continued as usual.

Doctors remained just as eager to prescribe speed. Many of them had obviously not kept up with the medical journals, which by the 1950s had not only noticed the addictive properties of speed but had also begun to warn about them. During the 1960s, doctors in the USA were writing 20 million prescriptions for speed each year, predominantly for weight reduction. This figure had risen to 31 million prescriptions by 1967. During the late 1950s, physicians were also starting to prescribe liquid methamphetamine for intravenous injection, as a treatment for registered heroin addicts.

Although speed pills used to be the magic bullets in a doctor's armoury and were prescribed by the millions, the therapeutic use of speed today is very limited, both in scope and in quantity. It is now only in exceptional circumstances and usually in small doses that speed is regarded as a therapeutic drug. The main exception is Dexedrine, still prescribed in 5mg doses for people with rare forms of narcolepsy, and with hyperactive children who have acute difficulties in sustaining concentration. Its use as an anorexic agent or a promoter of weight reduction – once very widespread – is also strongly discouraged but can nonetheless be found in professions such as modelling where the desire to attain the "body beautiful" is still paramount.

FROM MEDICINE CABINET TO STREET

One of the great ironies of the twentieth century, is the way that many of today's street drugs have mutated from perfectly respectable medical treatments to vilified and demonized killers. The drugs themselves have not changed but the public's relationship with them has. There is very little appreciation in today's heavy anti-drugs climate that the majority of the substances that society now considers vanquishers of youth were dispensed by the medical profession in the first place. In fact, so often does a drug follow the route from wonder cure to deadly fix that the rational person has to strain to avoid the conclusion that there is a degree of purposefulness about it all – if only by way of a dogged short-sightedness.

As speed is a wholly synthetic drug, it does not have the long history of illicit use usually found with naturally occurring psychoactive drugs. However, during the twentieth century, the development of speed as a street drug was extremely rapid. It was a classic example of a drug that went "straight from the medicine cabinet to the street". True to its nickname, the use of speed expanded at a rapid pace.

The non-therapeutic use of Smith, Kline and French's Benzedrine Inhaler also became widespread. It was soon discovered that the contraption could be dismantled or broken open to remove the amphetamine-saturated wadding inside. This wadding was soaked in water, coffee or any other drink, to give a real kick. The B-Bomb, as it was dubbed, was jazz musician Charlie Parker's first contact with drugs. The use of inhaler preparations of speed became a significant problem in the USA during the 1940s. The only solution seemed to be the withdrawal of these preparations from the market, which came into effect in the 1950s.

The inhaler was just one of a growing number of products containing speed available in the 1930s and 1940s. This was a time of great economic depression followed by a horrific war, and it is no surprise that speed pills – also known as "brain" or "pep" pills – seemed to be the best aid to escaping or coping with the stress. Speed was the ideal pharmaceutical accessory to these troubled times.

SPEED WARRIORS

In addition to medicinal applications, speed was – and still is – used in two basic ways: firstly, it had a functional use, to combat sleepiness and increase short-term endurance when a physical or mental task needed to be accomplished; secondly, it was a very popular recreational drug, used by people to stay awake and increase their energy levels for the purpose of play, rather than work. During the 1930s, the world discovered speed as an "upper" and by the middle of that decade its non-medical use had become widespread. By the outbreak of the Second World War, such use had reached hitherto unparalleled proportions.

It was not only the ordinary members of the public who were using

A DIFFERENT KIND OF CHEMICAL WARFARE

speed to keep their morale up, the drug was soon being introduced by the military establishment. Speed, with all its useful properties, was too tempting for military chiefs to ignore. The first extensive non-medical application of speed was recorded in the Spanish Civil War when it was given to fighting troops to counter fatigue, reduce appetite and bolster confidence. The precedent was set.

During the Second World War, soldiers in all the fighting forces, both allied and axis, were liberally supplied with a full tool-kit of speed by their military leaders. The men needed something to boost their morale and combat their battle fatigue: speed was the answer. The drug was handed out almost as a supplement to their war rations. The exact amount of speed consumed by military personnel during the war has not been disclosed by all the governments concerned, but it is estimated today that the war-time intake of speed by the military ran into hundreds of millions of doses. Almost 72 million tablets were provided to British forces alone, prompting a London newspaper in 1941 to carry the bizarre headline "Methedrine wins the Battle of London". An estimated 200 million tablets were given out to American troops. Japanese kamikaze pilots flew their missions tanked up on speed and German Panzer troops used them to maintain their physical endurance.

BORN TO RUN WILD

During the 1950s, amphetamine dependence slowly came to be recognized by some in the medical establishment. Medical journals began to discuss the possible downside that this wonder drug could visit on the user. Patients who were prescribed amphetamines on a regular basis, to reduce appetite for example, complained to their doctors of depression or an inability to work when the drug was reduced or discontinued. But this was not widely publicized and there was no reduction in its use by the public. Speed was flexible and cheap enough to be taken at work or at home, in a bar or in a club, socially or even alone, for indiscriminate or occasional use. Who was going to report a friend or a colleague for using speed when, until very recently, anyone could buy these pills over the counter like sweets?

The use of speed by the American military increased once more when the USA found itself at war again, first in Korea and then in Vietnam. During the period 1966–69, at the height of the Vietnam War, the US Army used more speed than the combined armed forces of the USA and the UK had done in the Second World War. In 1969, the US military establishment was one of the largest purchasers of speed from pharmaceutical companies. Different forces seemed to require different levels of speed. The average sailor in the US Navy took the most, consuming the equivalent of 21 pills per person, per year. He was closely followed by the top-guns of the Air Force whose intake peaked at about 17.5 pills annually. US Army personnel were obviously able to get on with their jobs with relatively less assistance, taking a mere 13.8 pills per soldier.

The absence of a war created a problem. There was no longer a military requirement for the drug yet there were tonnes of speed available. Unlike the butter-mountains of later years, the vested interests in the pharmaceutical industry were desperate for a quick solution to their hungry search for profits from speed. The obvious answer lay in creating domestic markets to absorb the excess and, more importantly, to generate a continuing return for investors.

The US Government's now-we-do and now-we-don't approach to speed didn't cut any ice with many of the soldiers returning from war. They had used speed while abroad on military service and didn't see why they shouldn't use it when they were home. Not only did they spread the word about this invigorating drug, but they also continued to use speed in their everyday lives. Their message was heard loud and clear across the nation and soon all sorts of ordinary people began to use speed to pep up their lives. The drug has a pedigree among blue-collar workers dating back to the 1950s, when Korean War veterans-turned-truckers criss-crossed the nation blocked up to the eyeballs on speed.

MOTHER'S LITTLE HELPER

In the UK, many young women developed speed habits in the search for a way to keep their weight down. This stemmed from the relentless bombardment of unrealistic, media-fuelled notions that the "ideal woman" should be thin and sylph-like and should remain eternally young. The first "speed-freaks" were often tired and isolated housewives and mothers who were prescribed pills either as anti-depressants or as weight-reduction aids. Combined with the fact that speed gave youthful energy and supreme confidence, it was a winner of a wonder drug for women. In addition to the actual weight loss it produced, the euphoric effects of speed sometimes also made women *feel* thinner. The amphetamine pill became "mother's little helper". Rita Crowley, a young housewife in the 1950s, who was prescribed Durophet M pills to help her lose weight, remembers the experience for all the other effects that speed had on her and her friends:

"We used to call them 'black bombers'. They worked. You couldn't eat anything when you were on them and if you were a smoker, you never stopped smoking. You were smoked dry – like a kipper. You couldn't sit still for a moment in the day. You just kept on – go, go, go. My curtains have never been up and down so much as when I was on those pills – but then my house has never been as clean,

either. I passed them on to my neighbours when any of them were feeling tired or a bit down. I remember giving some to one particular friend once. She was on such a roll that she was getting her kids up at 3 in the morning to wash the sheets!"

Soon women began to use them not only as a diet pill and an aid to housework, but also as a pick-me-up and as an antidote to the loneliness and drudgery of being stuck at home with nothing but chores to do. They were eagerly sought after as a fillip to cope with the mental and physical exhaustion that arose from having too much housework combined with a lack of intellectual stimulation from anyone over the age of three.

But Dr George Birdwood, a National Health Service general physician (GP) practising at that time, remembers picking up the pieces:

"In the short term, the women were helped to an extent by the pills. But in the long run, they came back to being as big as they were before and as miserable as they were before except now they were stuck with a drug habit."

THE PERFECT WIFE, THE PERFECT HOME, THE PERFECT PICK-ME-UP

In 1961, two and a half per cent of all National Health Service prescriptions were for amphetamines. As a result of such widespread availability, the UK Government introduced the Drugs (Prevention of Misuse) Act in 1964, which made unlicensed possession and importation of amphetamine an offence. Punishing the end-user for possession did nothing to restrict the drug's manufacture, storage or prescription, however. The UK Government expected constraints to come from within the pharmaceutical industry and the medical profession. But the changes were cosmetic: a colour alteration here and a change of shape there. This was yet another green-light to the pharmaceutical manufacturing industry to continue the mass-production of a substance that was now known to be highly addictive. Confronted by the day-to-day concerns of their patients, doctors continued to prescribe speed.

Boss Goodman, roadie to the Pink Fairies, recalls his youth as a chubby young school-leaver in the early 1960s when, along with many others, he was prescribed black speed pills by his doctor to lose weight:

"When I started taking those pills I became the fastest supermarket shelf stacker in the West! And then one day my boss told me exactly what it was that I was taking and I wanted some more. So I went to my doctor and told him that I didn't have enough and that I needed more. He didn't ask any questions, he just wrote out the script (prescription). If he hadn't given it to me, I'd have gone down the road and got it from another doctor 'coz everyone was at it."

The unregulated and indiscriminate prescription of speed continued for some years in the UK. A staggering four million prescriptions were issued in 1966 alone. By 1967, this had declined to 2.5 million prescriptions. But this was still a very high number, given the fact that by now the medical establishment was almost unanimous in its agreement that speed had very little therapeutic value. This trend carried on until early 1969, when warning bells rang for Dr Frank Wells, a worried local Ipswich GP.

Dr Wells had found that the number of his patients coming back to him for repeat prescriptions of speed had increased almost twofold since he had begun his medical practice. Worried by this trend and the possibility of addiction, he turned to the medical journals and found confirmation for his fears. Academic medical circles had for some time been flagging up the dangerously addictive nature of chronic speed use. He took his findings to a meeting of local GPs and asked if they would agree a temporary ban on the prescription of speed and see how their patients fared. Many of their patients were very unhappy, some threatened to change doctors, some actually did change doctors, but most stayed and seemed to cope without the drug. The habit was quite easily broken, with few unpleasant side effects. This voluntary ban among the Ipswich physicians caught the attention of the medical establishment and the media and, over time, this encouraged a national trend toward a reduction in speed prescriptions.

ILLEGAL MANUFACTURE

The impact of the mass-marketing and over-prescription of the previous two decades ensured that a large percentage of the population had developed a real taste for speed – a taste that wasn't going to go away or be displaced by the medical profession's new-found conscience. The huge demand led to the development of an illegal manufacturing industry on a global scale. Illicitly manufactured speed exists in four main forms. For reasons that are unclear, these different forms of illicit speed are more popular in some parts of the world than others.

Illicitly manufactured and distributed speed powder or amphetamine sulphate is known as "sulph", "biker sulph", or "whizz" and is much more frequently encountered in Europe. Injectable speed or illicit methamphetamine hydrochloride is known by names such as "meth", "crystal" and "crank" and there is also a highly potent smokable form of methamphetamine hydrochloride, most commonly known as "ice". Both of these forms are much more common in Asia and North America. In addition to the original speed compounds, numerous derivatives have been developed – some used on their own and some mixed with vitamins or CNS depressants.

AMPHETAMINE SULPHATE

By far the most common form of street speed since the seventies has been amphetamine sulphate, an off-white or pinkish powder containing equal amounts of laevoamphetamine and dexamphetamine. Historically, it has always been "cut" or diluted with other components. Most of the illicit speed used by young people in the UK is in the form of amphetamine sulphate, with an average purity of no more than five per cent. The rest of the mixture is usually made up of less powerful stimulants such as caffeine, ephedrine, non-stimulant drugs such as paracetamol (US acetaminophen) or totally inert substances like glucose or Vitamin C. Occasionally, chalk, talcum powder or other fillers are used, causing serious damage if injected, as these substances clot inside the veins. It has even been known for crushed glass to be found cut in with speed.

Sulphate is typically sniffed but it has also been known to be swallowed with a drink. However, with purity at such low levels, the injecting of speed is widespread, as users try to maximize the effects of the drug. Individual use often varies greatly. An occasional snorter of speed might take quite some time to consume half a gram but a heavy and regular user with a very high tolerance level could consume up to eight grams a day. Prices vary enormously, but sulphate can cost anything from £20 a gram down to as little as £8 a gram. The powder is also sold in £5 "wraps" containing approximately half a gram, with only about 25mg of real speed.

SPEED BASE

Amphetamine "base" is also used in the UK, but to a much lesser extent than sulphate. Base is a lumpy, greyish-white paste, of between 40 and 60 per cent purity. It is just a step along the way in the process to producing the powder. In the main it is used orally, but there are always some elements, as with any other drug, that inject it or smoke it. The price of amphetamine base seems to be double that of sulphate or powdered speed. The relative strength of base, as compared to sulphate, caused many people at one time to think that it was a clever marketing device being used by speed dealers to soften up users for another much more expensive kind of base – cocaine base or "crack".

"CRANK" CALLS

In the late 1950s, some doctors in the USA began to prescribe liquid speed or methamphetamine to be administered intravenously as a treatment for – and alternative to – heroin addiction. Other doctors and pharmacists became involved in writing illegal prescriptions for liquid speed vials. These practices contributed to the development of new patterns of use involving injectable speed. The most popular brands were made by Abbott (Desoxyn) and Burroughs Wellcome (Methedrine). During the first six months of 1962, over half a million vials of the drug were prescribed to patients.

One consequence of the excessive production of pharmaceutical grade speed, combined with its widespread popularity, was the development of a thriving black market. This involved diverting large quantities of speed from pharmaceutical companies, wholesalers, pharmacists and physicians. It is estimated that up until 1971, one half to two thirds of the 100,000 pounds of pharmaceutical speed produced each year in the USA was diverted to the black market and into the hands of chronic users.

The use of injectable speed spread to a variety of groups throughout the San Francisco Bay area. Particular pockets of the speed scene soon became notorious. The area called Haight-Ashbury was a microcosm of everything that epitomized the 1960s' drug sub-culture. Liquid speed slowly began to replace hallucinogenic drugs such as LSD as the "new guys on the block". The switch from LSD to speed in the popularity stakes first appeared in this part of town. Intravenous speed use, combined with the inevitable increased tolerance to the drug, escalated its use. San Francisco was the bed from which arose the term "speed-freak", first coined to refer to heavy intravenous users. The world-famous public campaign in response to this worrying trend warned that "speed kills".

The American Department of Justice slowly became aware of the magnitude of the illegal prescription scam and forced manufacturers and doctors to take action to curb the trend. Under pressure in the USA, Abbott withdrew Desoxyn in 1962 and Burroughs Wellcome withdrew Methedrine in 1963. By 1963, the success of US government measures to eliminate pharmaceutical vials of speed from the street had had a big impact on injectors, who were used to the purity of this product. It left intravenous users floundering without a product that could be readily injected. Demand was thus

San Francisco's Haight-Ashbury quarter

created for an inexpensive water-soluble powder product. A starved market led to a heightened demand, resulting in the first illicitly manufactured water-soluble methamphetamine powder – otherwise known as "crank".

What resulted was the emergence of the first illicit "bathtub" speed laboratories in late 1962 in the San Francisco area to satisfy the demand for a user-friendly product. Illegal laboratories ranged from one-room operations producing a few grams (ounces) of amphetamine per week to full-scale, highly organized groups producing 11kg (25lb) per week. This illicit speed quickly filled the void created by the scarcity of legally produced speed. The product came to be known by a number of street names, apart from "crank", such as "bathtub crank", "biker crank", "peanut-butter" and "wire". As its most common street name suggests, this form of injectable speed crank was intended to take hold of the body and "crank it up". It's ability to deliver a swift and very hard rush to the system was much in demand. Illicit crank began to be – and still is – manufactured in significant quantities in clandestine laboratories. With the escalation of use during the 1960s came an increase in violence and a diffusion of the illicit manufacturing and distribution of speed outward from Haight-Ashbury to the rest of the West Coast.

Crank has been popular in the American Midwest since the late 1960s, controlled by white outlaw motorcycle gangs. Crank came to be regarded as the best speed for the biker lifestyle, which emphasized fast, high-risk motorcycling, regular fighting, heavy drinking and constant partying. These gangs, realizing there was a profit to be made, began manufacturing and distributing the drug. The combination of their affinity for speed and the sizeable profits to be made led to their increasing involvement in, and dominance over, its manufacture and distribution by the early 1960s.

After cannabis, crank is the second most prevalent illicit drug in America. In fact, according to Bob Weiner, the spokesperson for the US drug "Czar", Barry McCafferey, crank is shaping up to be the crack of the twenty-first century.

During the late 1960s, there was a small and short-lived "outbreak" of intravenous speed use in the UK. This was not among pill users who had graduated to the needle, but among an existing group of heroin and cocaine users who had been forcibly switched to oral methadone after GPs were banned from prescribing cocaine and heroin. Methedrine allowed them to continue to use a needle, something of a compulsion for intravenous users. This didn't last for very long. Within a year, the prescription of Methedrine was also controlled by the authorities. As a result of this latest hurdle in the supply of injectable speed, users turned to the street for Chinese White – the illicit heroin that had begun to make its way to London from Hong Kong.

ICE CRYSTALS

The heavily concentrated, high-potency, high-purity, crystallized form of methamphetamine, smoked as opposed to injected, is more commonly known as "ice" on the street. It is produced by re-crystallizing methamphetamine powder. For users, one of the main attractions of ice is that it is enormously difficult to adulterate. One user described its appearance this way: *"Looks kinda like rock salt, clear. Almost like rock candy. Some can be big, like a diamond, looks almost like diamonds!"* In Hawaii, the drug is almost exclusively smoked in a glass pipe. The inhalation of the vapours leads to rapid absorption into the bloodstream and dissemination to the brain, resulting in a very powerful rush. There is an immediate onset of effects, similar to those experienced by injecting users, only much stronger. The pattern of use that emerged in Hawaii was one of "bingeing and crashing", or continuous smoking in runs of three to eight days, followed by complete exhaustion, where the user sleeps for prolonged periods. Ice was developed and distributed independently from the US mainland methamphetamine networks. For many years, law enforcement officials in Hawaii assumed that ice was an entirely different drug from methamphetamine.

The earliest reports of ice in Honolulu date back to the late 1970s, but it was during the mid and late 1980s that ice was identified by Hawaiian law enforcement sources as being in very widespread use. By 1989, it had reached epidemic proportions and the news of a drug potentially more dangerous than crack appeared in headlines across the country and in mainland USA.

As one user stated, by 1990, ice was available anywhere on the islands: *"When I went in jail in 1987, it didn't seem it was that rampant. But when I came out at the beginning of 1990, it was everywhere. It was like an epidemic! Everywhere you turned, everybody was smoking it."*

One factor more than any other seems to account for its rapid rise in Hawaii. Hawaii had long been noted as a centre for very high quality cannabis. Tourist memorabilia such as T-shirts, key chains, baseball caps and posters boasted of the locally grown and internationally famous "Kona gold". In local family circles, cannabis was perceived to be a harmless mild relaxant, used widely and openly. Local law enforcement agencies, pushed by the narcotics agencies of mainland USA, launched an intensive cannabis eradication campaign, which resulted in the destruction of large and small-scale production of cannabis weed and transformed the illicit drug economy of Hawaii. The eradication campaign against cannabis left local residents without their customary, and some would say benign, smoke. As a result, cannabis smokers, denied their drug of choice, were pulled toward a different and more dangerous kind of smoke by an extremely well-organized marketing campaign by the Asian manufacturers and distributors of the drug.

According to the *1999 Global Illicit Drug Trends Report*, from the United Nations Office for Drug Control and Crime Prevention, methamphetamine (both crank and ice) continues to be mainly associated with North America and East Asia, while amphetamine (sulphate and base) remains dominant in Europe.

OTHER AMPHETAMINE-LIKE STIMULANTS

In the light of the concern that speed has caused over the years it is worth looking at other amphetamine-like substances now being prescribed for medicinal uses. The main speed-related substances are listed below:

Ritalin: Closely related structurally to amphetamine, Ritalin is a less potent stimulator of the CNS – a quality that made it a drug preferred by doctors for treating hyperactive children. In adults it was prescribed for listless, senile behaviour, mild depression and narcolepsy. In virtually every respect, the drug produces the same adverse and positive effects as amphetamine, though of slightly lesser magnitude, dose for dose. Street users have often described Ritalin as a "cleaner high" and it was especially fashionable among serious "poly-drug" users who injected it as a companion to a "downer" (barbiturates). It was also mixed with the painkiller Diconal to make a speedball substitute. So popular did it become in unauthorized circles that, in 1983, it was withdrawn and is now rarely seen in the UK.

But the story is very different in the USA. In 1970, according to Dr Ronald Lipman of the Federal Drug Enforcement Agency (FDEA), as many as two-hundred thousand so-called hyperactive children were being treated with Ritalin. However, a follow up study of 83 teenagers showed that while 60 per cent of them showed some overall improvement, over 75 per cent still showed poor concentration, impulsiveness and defiance, and 25 per cent of them were involved in antisocial activities. Low self-esteem, worthlessness and difficulties with schoolwork also persisted.

As a result of a few studies that arrived at similar findings and conclusions with Ritalin, it was advised by the FDEA that the use of this drug be drastically cut down. But by the 1990s, Ritalin was at the centre of a 1990s controversy surrounding its over prescription for hyperactive children and there are reports in both the lay press and in medical journals suggesting that Ritalin might have serious side-effects that doctors have not taken into consideration. The panic seems to be the greater because it is children who, in the main, are being prescribed this drug.

Diethylproprion: A moderately less potent version of amphetamine, diethylproprion has been one of the most commonly prescribed slimming drugs, despite strong official warnings against issuing it in any circumstances. The various branded versions have had a strong tradition of street use. Apisate and Tenuate Dospan are still available.

Khat: The stems and leaves of the shrub *Catha edulis* contain a number of psychoactive chemicals, and can be chewed or made into tea. The most powerful constituent is cathinone, an amphetamine-like stimulant, that is extremely unstable and breaks down spontaneously within days of the plant being picked. Cathinone is prohibited under the Misuse of Drugs Act (1971), but Khat itself is not a prohibited substance.

The shrub is cultivated over large areas of East Africa, where chewing the leaves has been customary for centuries. Like coca leaves, they induce a sense of energy and well-being, but are also prone to cause stomach upsets, irritability, or sleeplessness. Their use has also been associated with oral cancer and liver disease, but it is difficult to tease out a direct effect from that of detrimental environmental conditions. The risk of psychosis and compulsive use is well recognized locally. Unless the leaves are fresh, diarrhoea is likely to be the only consequence noted by the consumer.

Nonetheless, khat has been the subject of some old-fashioned media scare stories, not least in London's *Time Out* magazine, which, in November 1993, ran a two-page item called "Deadly Harvest" that described how a large proportion of London's Somali population were "chewing non-stop for fifteen hours at a time". The piece reported that during the last three decades, "use of the drug has exploded in Somalia in particular where it is generally credited with exacerbating the civil war, crippling the economy and producing a work-shy generation of living zombies."

Among a group of Somalis living in London, 75 per cent of those interviewed had used khat in the past and 86 per cent of these were still current users. On average this would happen in the evening three times a week, usually in a social context. The leaves are sold in bundles costing £4, and the average consumption was seven bundles a month. Adults questioned would much prefer their children to use khat than alcohol or cigarettes.

Unwanted effects were common but generally mild and included sleep disturbances, reduced appetite, mood swings, anxiety and panic, depression and irritability. Dependency upon khat appeared unusual, but many people admitted using more in London than they had in Somalia.

Pemoline: Less potent than amphetamine, its main prescribed use is to treat hyperactive children. Less often it is used to counter the sleepiness of people being treated for severe pain with morphine and other opioids. Claimed by street users to stimulate the memory and the loins, the current branded product is called Volatil. Users claim that they can remember almost anything said to them – or even seen – only once. Much more importantly, people seem to value it for its ability to allow the user to engage in sexual relations for as long as they want, without feeling all the normal human exhaustion of extended love-making.

THE FAUSTIAN PACT

The word "drug" – whether or not you are referring to a psychoactive chemical – still means what Hippocrates and Galen, the fathers of scientific medicine, understood it to mean many hundreds of years ago. It is a substance that instead of being "overcome" by the body, is instead capable of "overcoming" the body, while provoking – in ridiculously small doses as compared to other foods – large changes: organic, or in mood, or in both.

The Greeks coined a rather subtle term to describe these substances: *pharmakon* – a word that means both remedy and poison, since one can so easily become the other, depending on the circumstances, the individuals and the knowledge they have. It is significant that just by changing the final letter of the word, to make *pharmakos*, the meaning changes to "scapegoat". Far from being a coincidence, this demonstrates that the Greeks were perfectly aware of the possible consequences of intoxicating excess!

THE PLEASURE PRINCIPLE

All potentially addictive drugs operate via the pleasure/reward system in the body. The pleasure/reward centre is a cluster of neurones situated at the heart of both frontal lobes of the brain. It exists in the most primitive mammals and in humans triggers feelings of well-being and content. A desire for an "altered consciousness" has always represented more to human beings than mere hedonistic self-indulgence. It is a basic human appetite recognizable throughout history from the most primitive times.

Consider alcohol, so widely available today. The use of alcoholic beverages dates back to our earliest ancestors and became associated with the worship of gods and demons. One of the most powerful Greek gods was Dionysus, god of wine. The Romans adopted Dionysus into their religion, but changed his name to Bacchus. Festivals and holidays associated with Bacchus celebrated the harvest and origins of life. Time has blurred the debauchery of Bacchanalian celebrations, but the assumption that drunkenness is an intrinsic part of public festivities has survived the pagan gods and remains a familiar theme in modern society. The term "Bacchanalian festival" now suggests a more appealing image than "drunken orgy", "pot party" or "speed run" but, whatever the label, the result is essentially the same.

If you ask today's teenagers why they use drugs, many will tell you that it is because these substances are pleasurable or exciting. Other reasons they might offer include a need to overcome feelings of shyness, anxiety or lack of confidence, or to fit in with friends. Some may even say that drugs make them feel sophisticated or pleasantly rebellious and independent. For many years, scientists have attempted to catalogue these explanations and attach numbers to them. One investigator said that over half the stated reasons for drug use were "fun and curiosity", a third claimed "peer pressure" and only a fifth attributed it to a desire for self-medication against some form of youthful angst. In the case of speed, the link between youth and drugs can be traced back to the rapid social changes of the 1950s, and the emergence of the "teenager" as a powerful social phenomenon.

ROCK 'N' ROLL GENERATION

The 1950s saw a new generation of disaffected, alienated youth both in the USA and the UK, kicking out against what their parents saw as the trophies of their victory over the axis powers – peace, safety and prosperity. For many youngsters of the period, this meant a bland meaningless world where passions were stifled and the pace of life beat to the tick of the factory clock. The UK was still austere and gloomy, life seemed to be black and white, rationing did not end with the war, the depressing sight of war damage was clearly visible all around and young people in the early part of the decade were aware that they did not enjoy the same economic freedoms as their American counterparts.

In the USA at the time, the stifling cloak of conformity throttled any kind of political radicalism in a wave of home-grown anti-communist hysteria. "Red" was the ultimate insult. In this respect at least, teenagers of all social classes did not differ from mainstream opinion. They weren't interested in revolution, because people got killed in real revolutions. What they wanted was safe rebellion – weekend unconventionality, crossing on to the wild side every so often, while on the way home to the comfort of Mom's Key-lime pie.

The term "adolescent" came from the language of sociologists and psychiatrists – "teenager" was an entirely different concept, born out of market research and the booming economics of consumerism. Before the

Second World War, those we now call "teenagers" existed in a demographic wilderness, not quite children, but with adulthood tantalizingly out of their reach. But by 1956 the teenager had become established as a cultural and commercial force in America. It was the year that rock 'n' roll came of age to give teenagers a voice and a prominence that no one could ignore any longer. The magic formula of rock 'n' roll mixed black rhythm and blues and urban blues with white country music and Southern gospel. And at the core of this new musical atomic

BUYING DRUGS IN THE '50s

explosion was a truck driver from Tupelo, Mississippi, Elvis Presley.

Much has been written and said about Presley over the years, but it's worth restating that he was an icon of the new age, the apotheosis of teenagers' fantasies the world over and of their parents' hates and fears. Half a century on, when so much has developed musically and culturally out of those early records, it is almost impossible to imagine the impact that people like Presley, Jerry Lee Lewis and Bill Haley had on a whole generation of young American kids hitherto brought up on Glenn Miller! Here were young white country boys, not crooning sickly-sweet ballads but belting out the words to earthy black music that left very little to the imagination. Unsurprisingly, because of its black influences, rock 'n' roll was roundly condemned by "red-necks" and their kind the length and breadth of the country in exactly the same terms as Jazz had been before it. The North Alabama White Citizens Council declared that rock 'n' roll was a "conspiracy" against the white community. Others, not quite so complimentary, called it a "communicable disease".

But Presley, Marlon Brando and James Dean were a new breed of working class American anti-heroes These people were much more potent symbols than the black jazz hipster, because they were white and thus were embraced and lionized by the media, which ensured their bankability. Their attitude was instantly recognizable; the sneer, the curling lip, the cynicism and the black leather jacket said it all.

GOING WILD

Speed informed the philosophy of youth culture in America; wheels were the essence of the 1950s experience – bombing up and down the vast highways of the country in the '49 Ford, the '55 Chevy, the T-bird or the Studebaker. Marlon Brando rode a bike in *The Wild Ones* and Jimmy Dean drove to screen immortality behind the wheel of his Porsche. But speed meant more than just zero to sixty in seconds. Rock 'n' roll needed a souped-up engine and heavy duty fuel to keep it going – new music and a new generation demanded new ways of getting stoned.

Neither rock 'n' roll nor the mod or garage bands of the 1960s, northern soul or punk in the 1970s can be legitimately considered outside the context of speed. The same logic applies to West Coast rock and acid and to marijuana and reggae. Certain drugs influenced the sound and creative context of particular genres of music more than others, but as the pharmaceutical industry became more competitive and street chemists more sophisticated, more drugs were added to the musical pharmacopoeia.

Back home after the war, American GIs brought their government-issue speed habits with them. Those who couldn't face the sheer monotony of life on the factory floor took to the freeways as truck drivers, transporting the fruits of the USA's post-war prosperity across the country. Amphetamine became the truck driver's friend. On speed, they needed less sleep and less food and they drove for much longer and, ultimately, more mileage meant more money.

While driving up and down the country, these truckers were hitting bars in the dusty towns of the south to hear country boys singing and to hear this new thing called rock 'n' roll. At the Wagon Wheel in Natchez, a young man called Jerry Lee Lewis played to the truckers, who showed their appreciation by tipping him with Benzedrine capsules.

Speed stood at the crossroads of early rock 'n' roll and country music, consumed by the performers, roadies and audiences alike. Johnny Cash got hooked on speed while touring across the country. At first, his performances were pin sharp, his timing spot on and he was bursting with confidence. But before long his voice was shot, he had a hungry, wasted look and his behaviour became violent and erratic.

THE ORIGINAL BURNOUT KIDS

These little magic pills also got rockers to gigs and gave them the confidence to tear these places apart. Years before the Who's speed-driven destructiveness and Hendrix's speed pyrotechnics with a burning Fender guitar, Jerry Lee Lewis set fire to his piano in 1958 screaming: *"I'd like to see any son of a bitch follow that!"* But even before Lewis, there was the original burnout guru in Hank Williams, acknowledged as one of the finest songwriters and performers that country music ever produced.

Country legend Hank Williams died of a heart attack at the age of twenty-nine, on New Year's Eve 1953. His speed intake had increased in direct proportion to his meteoric rise to fame, bursting on to the country music scene only four years before his death. It was a fame that this son of a lumber worker just could not handle. He did not die a tragic death to cement his legendary status – but in a sense his life and the lives of all those who screamed down the fast lane was defined through and by its temporary nature. Jerry Lee Lewis and Johnny Cash both fought long and arduous battles against speed. Cash found religion and was saved, but Lewis just kept right on, landing himself in more and more trouble.

Speed was only brought under strict federal control in 1970, but long before that, from 1951 Jerry Lee Lewis was falling foul of the existing legislation that controlled sales of non-prescription drugs. He and some of his entourage were caught with 700 capsules after their hotel room was raided in Grand Prairie, Texas. And that's how it went for the next twenty years. Constant speed use made Lewis unpredictable, violent and paranoiac, shooting off guns in hotel rooms and getting into other kinds of trouble.

BRITANNIA ROCKS

The history of speed and popular music takes us from the American Deep South to the south of England – or more specifically, to the club scene in London's West End. Up until the 1950s, notwithstanding the few hysterical newspaper outbursts about drug use, drug-taking in England was quite circumscribed and illicit drug use was not really a social issue yet. Most addicts were notified to the Home Office and received maintenance prescriptions from their GPs. Most were "therapeutic addicts" who had become hooked through GP prescriptions for pain relief, often for war injuries.

By the early 1960s, trends from across the Atlantic were starting to have an effect on a younger sector of UK society. The commercial and cultural concept of "youth" now existed as a separate entity for the first time in the eyes of the media and society at large. Apart from the mileage to be made from their outrageous and apparently deviant behaviour, the evolution of these sub-cultures also created separate consumer markets, which were pounced upon by eager entrepreneurs – selling everything from Levi jeans to an array of drugs. Two very different groups were involved in the fashion for casual speed use. Many young people, most notably members of the "mod" sub-culture, took "Drinamyl" and "Dexedrine", primarily to allow them to stay awake and dance in the all-night clubs of major cities such as Liverpool, Manchester and London, where the music scene was sparking off something new and wild for this audience.

The second group of active users were at the other end of the spectrum – older, intravenous heroin and cocaine addicts. They had been moved on to injecting methamphetamine by a rogue London doctor, who tried to get his patients off cocaine and heroin by switching them over to speed instead. For a very short time in the late 1960s, injectable Methedrine found its way on to London's illicit drug market.

Cultural changes tend to influence the types of drugs in circulation. In the late 1960s, people began to *feel* different – and how you *felt* began to matter like never before. As the culture changed, so the beat of the music followed suit and so, inevitably, did the drugs that were taken. The search was on for a different kind of "high" and by the end of the 1960s, the amphetamine scene seemed to die down. The new emphasis was on slowing down the experience of life, not speeding it up – on being able to escape to far away places in your own head without actually moving very far. The amazing psychedelic hippie wave took over and the order of the day was "chill out" as opposed to "pep up". Talking deeply for hours, rather than dancing yourself into a state of exhaustion, became the hip way to *be*. Speed seemed to become old hat and the magic of LSD took over. But, however intense the hippie trip was, it wasn't sustained for long.

By the mid 1970s, the craze for extra energy to dance the night away was back. This time it started with the northern soul clubs and then moved on to punk. Young people were now using illicitly manufactured speed as well as any legally manufactured speed pills they could get their hands on, even if it meant burgling chemist shops. Their goal was to find anything that was cheap and would help them stay up all night and dance to the inspirational new sounds of the moment.

Although speed and mods came to be almost mutually dependant, mods weren't the first sub-culture to start using them. Taking their cue from America, UK beatniks had been there long before the mods. Also social workers in the late 1950s noted fairly extensive use of Drinamyl, the blue triangular-shaped compounds of amphetamine and barbiturates, known more commonly as "purple hearts", among East End prostitutes.

Speed wasn't unknown with the working musicians of the time, either. Pills in different shapes and colours kept the pop and rock 'n' roll tours moving in the 1950s and 1960s. The Beatles consumed copious amounts of Preludin pills – speed, bought at the chemist's. Tanked up on these, they would play hour after hour, seven days a week at various clubs in Hamburg. 'Prellies' kept them awake, frantic enough to whip up the crowd and free from hunger. According to Peter Brown, former business manager of the Beatles: *"John was so out of control one night, that when a customer overenthusiastically approached the stage, John kicked him twice in the head and then grabbed a steak knife from the table and threw it at him."*

The Beatles discovered what the rock 'n' rollers already knew and what musicians of the future would soon find out – that speed was a "working drug". It works by giving the musician the courage to get out there and play as well as sufficient "edge" to keep going at full capacity throughout the performance. But trying to talk to the audience can be a mistake. When Elvis was taking large quantities of speed to try to trim down for a tour, some of his audiences were subjected to long rambling monologues from him between songs.

QUADROPHENIA

For the mods of the day, speed was symbolically enshrined at the heart of their sub-culture, fitting into a system that correlated with everything else; the clothes, the music, their scooters and their friends, all had a particular relationship with one another. Drugs were the adhesive that held together all their disparate frantic activities.

"Mod" was a catch-all phrase that encompassed a variety of styles contributing to a media-created image of "Swinging London". It should ideally have been called "Speeding London". The speed-induced arrogance, freneticism and edginess of the mod culture was reflected throughout the art, music and fashion of the times.

Speed promoted a sense of controlled anger among the mods – their stance was undeniably uptight. They looked normal but they weren't. In 1961, two and a half percent of all National Health Service prescriptions were for speed. Even so, mods made speed their very own. And it was this youthful casual use of speed, not just the over-prescription by GPs, that caused speed to be controlled in drugs

MODS – RUNNING WITH THE FAST CROWD

legislation, passed in 1964, that was created specifically for this drug.

The relentless pursuit of fashion eclipsed everything else; food, drink and women didn't matter, because speed killed the appetite for all three – which may account for the fact that the mod cult was predominantly male. Many mods had office jobs, earning money, most of which got spent on clothes and pills. A mod could spend a lot of his wages on changing the lapels of his mohair jacket or getting the right Church's brogues. Probably no other teenage style has paid so much attention to the detail of its threads – an obsession which reflected the way that speed users typically got totally absorbed and obsessed by mindless and trivial pursuits.

In the UK, the club scene has always provided a key platform for the development of new genres of musical taste. That's where good new music was to be found and also the drugs. Dark, subterranean dives, packed with young people dancing frantically to loud music, were an ideal setting for drug dealing. One of the main centres for speed dealing was the Scene Club – run as part of the infamous Nash gang's Soho operation. Two men who manned the door for a while had a habit of relieving patrons of their speed stash, pretending to flush it all down the loo and then recycling it. Dealing went on inside the clubs – safe from prying eyes.

Dr Sam Hutt, a young clubber in those days, remembers what happened when the police checked the clubs for drugs:

"One minute you'd be dancing madly to the music and the next minute the record would screech to a halt and the club manager or someone else would get up to the mike and say 'Meat van outside, meat van outside'. Everybody knew what that meant. The next

minute you'd hear this noise like a roll of muted thunder and everyone was dropping the pills from their pockets on to the floor. The police were hardly going to arrest everyone in the club!"

The clubs where speed was used and dealt ranged from the world famous to the fly-by-night. Despite it's clean image, the Marquee was a pill palace. The all-nighter sessions at the Flamingo gave mods a chance to hang with black American air force men on passes and dance to the black-inspired rhythm and blues of Georgie Fame and the like. Mods also went to clubs like the Last Chance, Le Kilt, La Poubelle, Roaring Twenties and Tiles. The music that was playing in these clubs wasn't of any one genre necessarily. Mainly it was the music that mods liked. But if any music came to represent the anger, frustration and arrogance of the mods, it was that of the Who.

From the very beginning, no one could beat the Who at being *the* mod band. No one could compete with Pete Townshend's anthems for a teenage wasteland and the Who's destructiveness. The audience responded to the Who on a number of levels but, primarily, it was the aggression, spurred on by their speed use: *"We were all pillheads,"* said Roger Daltrey. *"We were probably the most aggressive group that's ever happened in England."*

Toward the end of the mod sub-culture, it was the Small Faces who carried the torch. Unlike the Who, the Small Faces were genuine mods, who assumed cult status on the London club scene. Even though their single "What 'Cha Gonna Do About It" reached number 14 in the charts in 1965 and in 1966 they had major success with "Sha La La La Lee", it was their 1967 single "Here Comes the Nice" that really epitomized them. In the very middle of the psychedelic revolution in London, with its hippies and its acid, the Small Faces brought out an anthem to the speed dealer and the pill-popping mod scene. They calmly strolled out on to "Top of the Pops" with:

"Here comes the Nice
He knows what I need
He's always there when I need some speed."

As Stevie Marriott said later: *"'Here Comes the Nice' was a drug song, but no one sussed it. And for us, the whole point being if they don't suss it, it's cool.... We could do it on 'Top of the Pops' and we did it to be rebellious in a way – to see what we could get away with."*

But speed also had very functional uses for mods. Speed meant they could stay awake all night and dance and it also gave them the energy to fight. After all, they had to be present at the ubiquitous mod-rocker clashes that were reported in all the papers at that time – appearances had to be kept up. But like anyone else on speed, mods faced the inevitable come-down, too. A favourite spot for young London mods to deal with the obligatory crash was a spot in Southend called "come-down hill". Boss Goodman describes the scene like this:

"Come-down hill was our place. We would get on our scooters and jet down to Southend and then just crash. If you weren't coming down off speed and you came there, you'd see this really funny sight of rows and rows of scooters and beyond them hundreds of mods all sat on this hill with their heads hanging and groaning really loudly because the speed had disappeared from our systems and it was horrible. We were a sorry sight. But mind you, this didn't put us off our plans to do exactly the same thing again."

It is unlikely that any mod could keep up a regime like this for very long, however much speed he took. It all cost money and although mods were the most affluent teenagers to date, the money had to run out some time. Nevertheless, Boss Goodman's diary does show us the importance of music and the club scene to all mods, whether they were hard-core or just weekenders.

HOTEL CALIFORNIA

During the 1960s, the Haight-Ashbury district of San Francisco, on the Californian west coast, was witnessing the beginnings of a speed/heroin crisis. The poet Allan Ginsberg's reaction to the increasing use of speed by young washed-out hippies in 1967 was one of shock. In an interview to the *Los Angeles Free Press* he said: *"Let's issue a general declaration to all the underground community: contra speedamos ex cathedra. Speed is antisocial, paranoid making. It's a drag – bad for your body, bad for your mind, in the long run uncreative and plague in the whole dope industry."*

By early 1971, speed use had reached such an extent that Larry Clark, director of *Kids* had enough material to publish *Tulsa*, a book of photographs depicting teenage speed freaks in the city. It was from this crisis that there developed the "Speed Kills" campaign, which grew up on the West Coast. The Haight-Ashbury Free Clinic was set up to deal with all the drug casualties of the time. They received money from the Monterey Music Festival and Bill Graham put on a number of benefit gigs to raise money for the clinic.

Strictly speaking, speed "kills" only very rarely, but it was an effective slogan around which to rally support and money from the music business. An information service called Do It Now was set up in Hollywood to give out accurate information to users. Radio stations allocated slots and musicians would speak on the various dangers of drugs. Frank Zappa once featured in a slot, saying: *"I would like to suggest that you don't use speed and here's why: it will mess up your liver, your kidneys, rot out your mind: in general, this drug will make you just like your father and mother."*

HIGH ENERGY AND HIPPIES WERE NO LONGER WORLDS APART

Zappa must have reckoned that if the threat of becoming like their parents didn't put the youth off drugs, nothing else would! Do It Now also knocked on the doors of several record companies asking them to donate tracks for an album that would help their cause. This record was called "First Vibrations" and some of the tracks featured were "Amphetamine Annie", "The Pusher", "Flying on the Ground is Wrong" and "Artificial Energy".

By the 1970s cocaine began to replace speed as the favoured stimulant of those with money to spend. But for those musicians who still considered themselves the spokesmen of American rock, whose music demanded a real jagged edge, and of course for those fans who could not afford cocaine, speed remained very much an important and integral part of their culture.

SOUL NIGHTS

Another kind of music that was making it big in America during the 1970s was soul. Record labels such as, Stax, Atlantic and Tamla Motown all exploded on to the music scene in the mid 1960s and soul's massive popularity ensured that it was only a matter of time before it made its way across the Atlantic to invade UK shores. Wedged in between all the big record label names was a far less commercial sound that was being played in the clubs – the sound of northern soul. This was an obscure, but infectious type of soul music that was beginning to take off in clubs – similar to Tamla Motown, but with a less engineered sound and a raw energy and edge.

This was soul music made for dancing. It had been around since its introduction in the 1960s and its popularity had slowly moved to the Midlands and the North of England where it found an eager and receptive audience. A network of clubs in towns such as Birmingham, Wolverhampton, Manchester, Stoke, Blackpool and Wigan, to name but a few, created a unique underground scene. Clubs like the Torch, the Twisted Wheel, the Wigan Casino and the Highland Rooms staged soul all-nighters where young people came to dance the night away. The overwhelmingly young population involved in northern soul needed to find a way out of the depression slowly taking over the UK in the seventies. Speed gave them the edge they needed to rise above all the pain and frustration of a country losing its way. Just like their mod forebears, the northern soulsters wanted energy to dance all night – and a guaranteed way they could get that energy was to use speed. Affordable, easily available and with the required reputation behind it – speed fitted perfectly into this scene.

By 1974, "northern soul" was the buzzword. It was breaking new ground with a sound all of its own. Slowly, the commercial angle crept in and members of the music industry started to turn up at various all-nighters to see if they could pick up any talent. The people from Blues and Soul were up at the Wigan Casino practically every week. Television cameras began to appear, curious to find out what all the fuss was about. As the scene was almost entirely fuelled by speed, it was difficult to keep a low profile with all that energy flying around.

Jobs became hard to hold on to if you were a regular dedicated northern soulster. When the choice was between sticking with the all-nighters or doing the sensible thing and walking away while you were ahead – not many fans took the sensible route. Ordinary working people who became "hooked" on northern soul, started slowly. First they got into the music, then they got into the clubs and the all-nighters, and then they started taking "a bit of this and a bit of that", and suddenly they were under pressure. Out-and-out weekenders were taking time off on a Monday to deal with the speed crash and catch up on all the sleep they had lost over the previous two days of partying. Soon their jobs took second place.

Many fans will tell you that there is no clear answer as to why northern soul was so popular. It remains a mystery for many of them. Pete McKenna, a northern soul devotee tries to explain it like this: "*It had a magic, a feel, an atmosphere, a rawness and a fuck off driving beat that buried everything else. It felt right to the ears and the body. Just right.*"

Before long, the police had cottoned on to what was happening and were everywhere. They would be waiting near the clubs at night, or more often in the morning, to catch the clubbers with their speed. Toward the end of 1974, there was a shortage of good quality speed to be had around the north and north-west, the heart of the northern soul scene. The lack of "good gear" made everybody tense. "Bad gear" could ruin a person's night out, and this began to happen to many a dedicated soulster. Soon, those who had been used to good gear and good nights out gave up on the clubs as they had become too dangerous to frequent.

HARD AS METAL – SMOOTH AS VELVET

Heavy metal had always been home to speed since the days of Blue Cheer, a key band of the West Coast speed scene, but it slipped from the public gaze in the mid 1970s. However, in the 1980s, it enjoyed a come-back both in the USA and the UK. In Britain, it was spearheaded by Motorhead. They were the classic advertisement for speed taking. Everything about the band was fast, their name (American slang for a speed freak), their music and their leading light, Lemmy, guitarist, singer and self-confessed lover of speed. Lemmy had been thrown out of Hawkwind after he was caught with a large quantity of the white powder in Canada.

He returned to the UK and put together Motorhead. Their album titles, "Overkill", "Iron Fist" and "No Sleep Till Hammersmith" left little to the imagination. In Lemmy's own words: *"My favourite drug is speed 'cause it gets me up on stage in a good mood, but I really wouldn't recommend it to most people because most people who do it go over the top, given a couple of weeks on it. It's not good for most people, but my metabolism seems to have adjusted."*

In the UK, Motorhead were coming up just at the time when punk rock was establishing itself and there was a good deal of cross-fertilization between the two styles, both feeding off the energy of the other. Often Motorhead would appear on the same bill as punk bands such as the Adverts and the Damned. But Motorhead stayed away from the strong tradition of heroin worship that was becoming part of the punk scene, thanks largely to the legacy of nihilism passed on by the genuinely talented Lou Reed and the Velvet Underground. The hippie dream was dying and Reed's bleak, hopeless view of urban life still lived – drugs are sickness and love, life and death.

Each Velvet song used notes that kept banging against each other until the feedback – the speed shriek – was the only place left to go. The sound of the band was a complete aural presentation of the speed experience. Reed sang of a white boy going into Harlem to score heroin, in "Waiting for the Man", and of the all-consuming love affair between a heroin addict and his drug, in "Heroin". For writing songs like "Heroin", Reed got a reputation as one of the biggest junkies around. But his own comments on the subject have always been ambiguous – *"Just because I write about it, doesn't mean I do it."* But during a low period in his life in the mid 1970s, Reed did admit to shooting up quantities of speed. His 1973 track "Berlin", was about the doomed love affair between two speed-freaks. Over time, the Velvet Underground mantle was passed on to bands such as the New York Dolls and Johnny Thunders and the Heartbreakers.

The New York Dolls best typified the fusion of hard rock, the cult of bisexuality and the reckless pursuit of some kind of doomed intoxication that influenced British punk rock to a great extent. The band was formed in 1971 with vocalist David Johansen, guitarists Johnny Thunders and Sylvain Sylvain, bassist Arthur Kane and drummer Bill Murcia. It took them only a very short while to become the darlings of the New York club scene, following in the famous footsteps of the Velvet Underground. They also got a tremendous boost to their career when, in 1972, the Faces invited them to play at Wembley. But in November 1972, their drummer Bill Murcia died of an overdose of pills and alcohol in London.

In an interview he gave, Doll's bassist Arthur Kane bemoaned the fact that they were seen as a bunch of "transsexual junkies", conveniently forgetting that during the song "Looking For A Kiss", David Johansen would do the old Velvet Underground routine of pretending to use a hypodermic needle on stage, while backstage they were all doing it for real. Dee Dee Ramone of the Ramones writes in his autobiography that New York Dolls drummer Jerry Nolan, who used to inject a speed fix called Dioxin, would call on him regularly and ask him to go and buy drugs.

Listen to the Sex Pistols and you can quite plainly hear the basic rock 'n' roll riffs of the New York Dolls – but they were played harder and faster and were overlaid with snarling, cynical vocals. This wasn't a coincidence. Malcolm McLaren had been appointed as the manager of the New York Dolls in 1975. When he failed in his attempts to revitalize them, he returned to London to try again with a new band.

PUNK RULES OK

Every drug has its own unique nature. Heroin suited the jazz horns but speed was the only drug which had what it took to keep up with the kind of noise that punk was making. Speed fitted the rock solid beat and the big fat riffs that bands like the Sex Pistols and the Clash were producing. From the moment that the Pistols appeared on television, on the "Grundy Show", and swore in front of a whole nation – punk was unstoppable. Punks had bag loads of attitude and they liked the idea of sticking their size ten Doc Marten boots into the great and good everywhere. They had overthrown the commercial disco sounds of the decade with a music that was very different. This raises the classic "chicken and egg" question – did punk come first and speed fit it perfectly, or was speed there first and punk evolve out of the use of it? Either way, punk and speed went hand-in-hand and nothing could separate them.

Speed filled the breach for all the hippie-hating punks and seemed made for their kind of music. Punk music comprised short fast songs and speed was about a short fast experience. Also speed was "politically correct" as far as punks were concerned – it was a cheap, proletarian drug that offered self-esteem and social mobility – and was far removed from the bourgeois cocaine, also doing the rounds at the time.

The context in which punk sprang up in the UK was different from other post-war adolescent movements that had preceded it. Britain in the late 1970s was itself a very different place from the country it had been. Punk angst was directed not only at straight society, but also at the previous rock generation that, in its own time, had been considered subversive and anarchic. Independent record labels mushroomed, providing the only consistent outlet for home-grown punk products, as established record companies tended to keep away

SPEED AND PUNK – A MARRIAGE MADE IN HEAVEN

from punk bands. Like the record companies, most West End clubs also refused to allow punk bands to play their venues, as they were scared of what the bands and their fans would end up doing.

In early 1977, the Roxy club opened in London for just a hundred days. It devoted itself to punk bands, as they had nowhere else to play. Every punk band worth their salt played at the Roxy that year – including the Sex Pistols, the Clash, Billy Idol and Generation X, Polystyrene and Xrayspecs, Siousxie and the Banshees and the Slits. The Roxy soon began to attract large enthusiastic punk crowds and also a lot of attention from the tabloid press, which produced articles about what they saw as the extremes of the punk way of life – "Fear and Loathing at the Roxy". These young people, with all their anger and their excesses, outraged the establishment of the day.

A film made at the time by the Notting Hill DJ and film-maker Don Letts, "A Punk Rock Movie", chronicles the life of the Roxy and all the punks that appeared in her. An observational documentary, this film shows scenes of punks going into the loos at the club to shoot up speed, various people and bands popping different pills, young punks cutting themselves with razor blades and all of this juxtaposed with punk songs such as Siousxie and the Banshees' "Bad Shape" and Johnny Thunders' "Chinese Rocks".

In late 1977, the Clash were booked to play the Rainbow – the London equivalent of Madison Square Gardens. Punk had arrived. The dam had finally broken and nothing was going to stop the raging sound of mad, bad England. At that concert, it was all action. Everyone was on speed and there was no keeping them down. People were ripping up seats, projectiles were flying, there was madness and mayhem all around. Things were unpredictable – exactly like the fuel that was keeping this show on the road. Speed takes no prisoners and punk was no exception.

Punk fashion was just as anarchic and furious as the music. Fans and bands alike took to wearing their anger on their sleeves, on their faces and in their hair. The cut-up punk uniform seemed to derive from the throwaway and disposable garbage of a crumbling industrial and manufacturing society with no future. Safety pins and multicoloured spiky mohican hairstyles abounded. There was nothing flash about the punk uniform – it took its cues from the sexual ambiguities and fetishes of the Velvet Underground's sadomasochistic vision of glam rock. Shock value was everything to a real punk and shocking a nation was easy when you were on speed. The Pistols' "Anarchy in the UK" pretty much summed the scene up and Johnny Rotten was the role model of the speed-shot punk, with his spiky dyed red hair, death-white face, metal hanging from his ear lobes and his apparently wasted physique. He looked like a speed corpse.

Katherine Safferey, a young punk from Birmingham, who had developed a strong taste for speed, remembers in vivid detail what using it was like:

"Using speed was like tasting ground up razor blades straight off a toilet floor. It smelled foul; the stuff really does stink. After you took it, you could taste it for hours, like liquid vomit going down your throat. Honestly, it smelt like cat's urine. You could always tell if a speed dealer walked into the pub, 'coz you'd go, 'God, someone's wet themselves', and the next second you'd go, 'Oh, it's only Mr Big.' I honestly don't know why we punks loved the drug so, but love it we did."

Unlike the hippies before them, punks did not consider there was any particular mystique surrounding drugs. It wasn't just hippie introspection they disliked and scorned, they weren't in awe of their drugs of choice, either. If it didn't get you high then it was of no use. After a long ride on speed, many punks found that it just didn't have the old kick and so they began to inject it for a better and faster hit. But even this doesn't last for long, as Charles Shaar Murray recalls:

"I began to notice that my hair started getting really manky, my teeth started falling out, my skin looked awful and I started getting every cold, flu or other bug that was going around. I felt so low and depressed. The way it was explained to me was that there was so much speed in my body that it had packed up producing adrenaline, because it wasn't required. It had to adjust itself to naturally producing adrenaline again."

BARB-ED WIRED

After a period of injecting speed, punks needed something to ease the jagged, jittery edge that it gave them and so many of them switched to the more dangerous, but still very cheap, barbiturates or "downers", such as Tuinal and Seconal, to slow themselves down. Tom Conneelly, a young man who spent almost a decade on speed, recalls what it felt like moving from speed to "downers":

"Eventually your body rebels and sleep deprivation gets to you. You don't eat much when you're on speed, so physically you're malnourished. Your body is going on with no fuel in it. It was like having a broken mirror inside me and the shards of glass were sticking into me. That's what it felt like. Whenever I found myself in that situation, I would take some barbiturates. And barbiturates are such a seductive thing. Once you've taken a few, you forget all about the speed which seems to have no attraction anymore."

Barbiturates cushioned and eased the comedown from speed. They rounded everything off and made the world an easier place to deal with. Despite the warning signs, doctors were handing out millions of barbiturate prescriptions in the 1960s and 1970s as sedatives and sleeping pills.

What's more, they were not controlled under the Misuse of Drugs Act until the 1980s, despite the fact that barbiturates were potentially the most lethal of all mind-altering street drugs, regarding both overdose and withdrawal. These drugs were implicated in the deaths of Brian Jones, Jimi Hendrix and Al Wilson from Canned Heat. In the 1970s, barbs were killing up to two thousand people a year in the UK and those it didn't kill it scarred, causing the most horrific abscesses. A unique feature of barbs was that when they were injected, they burned the flesh from the inside, leaving gaping holes.

Barbs were cheap and accessible for the mass of young punks. But for the punk rock stars who had more money to spend, like Topper Headon or Keith Levene, there was always heroin to help take the edge off the speed crash. They fell into the ritual of heroin worship that had found its way to London from the New York club and music scene. The punk scene was tired now – it had "hurled itself against a brick wall" for years and wasn't going to escape undamaged. People were beginning to show signs of what was commonly known in punk circles as "fried brains". They had frazzled themselves out.

VICIOUS END

Sid Vicious, the main man of the Sex Pistols and "enfant terrible" of British punk died away from home in New York. Sid was an unknowing victim of what is called a "hot shot". The story goes that being accustomed to a New York heroin purity of no more than five per cent, Sid's metabolism was not prepared for the 30 per cent plus powder that was thoughtfully brought over for him from the UK. Although his eventual death had been caused by a massive heroin overdose, he had started his drug career many years before on the fuel that drove the punk nation – speed. Speaking in a BBC interview in the late 1970s, the punk icon admitted to having had a particularly heavy speed habit: *"I used to be a speed freak at one time before I joined the band. I used to deal loads of speed and I was also shooting speed all the time. I was doing anything up to 14 hits a day – I had track marks all down my arms."*

THE WAR
AGAINST SPEED

The clandestine manufacture and illicit supply of speed only dates back to the early 1960s. By the mid 1970s, clandestine laboratories were being detected in significant numbers each year. Slowly, the legal manufacture of amphetamine, which supplied some of the illicit market, dried up and the clandestine sector emerged as the main source of supply for the street market. Two main factors aided this development:

Firstly, speed is relatively simple to manufacture through chemical synthesis, and this encouraged many laboratory operators to enter the arena of illicit speed production, though it must be said that the quality of the drug differed greatly from laboratory to laboratory. Economies of scale don't play much part in the cost of speed production as even very small quantities can be manufactured profitably by choosing an appropriate method. This gives the manufacturing process a high degree of flexibility with regard to the sophistication of the drug and the quantities to be processed.

Secondly, in contrast to plant-based narcotics, illicit speed manufacturing is more difficult to monitor and therefore to control. Speed tends to be manufactured relatively close to the markets it supplies, which greatly reduces the risks associated with trafficking. This is especially true for crank. In the case of sulphate, it is more common to have a relatively centralized manufacturing base to serve a larger regional market – such as Europe. In addition, it is difficult to estimate and monitor the extent of synthetic drug manufacture because the precursors required for the process are easily and widely available and are seldom tied to a particular geographical area. This is in marked contrast to plant-based narcotics which are extracted from a naturally growing product that is cultivated openly, often in the same locations, over many years.

A COTTAGE INDUSTRY

Prior to 1962, supplies of speed came from pharmaceutical companies, which defined the quality and purity of the drug. After 1962, the availability and quality of the illicit product was rather more unpredictable. Up until 1974, only 30 per cent of street samples purporting to be the drug truly were speed. "Look-alike" speed flooded the street market. But from 1975 to 1983, the speed content of street samples slowly but surely increased from 60 to 90 per cent. The street chemists had been working very hard on perfecting their product. Over time, with the improvement both in quality and availability, illicitly manufactured speed came to dominate the street market.

THE HUMBLE BEGINNINGS OF A LUCRATIVE BUSINESS

Sites for laboratories varied from sophisticated, underground hideaways to hotel rooms, kitchens, bathrooms, garages or disused properties. The laboratories were often located in secluded rural areas at a safe distance from the metropolitan areas that they served, primarily to avoid the discovery of fumes and odours vented during the process. Laboratory operators ranged from high school drop-outs to chemists with degrees and doctorates. In many cases, the producers lacked sufficient knowledge and skill to synthesize the drug properly and completely. In these cases, the purity and quality of the drug suffered, with the end product containing high levels of contaminants.

Illicit laboratories were generally operated on an irregular basis. Manufacturers often produced a "batch" of a drug, then disassembled, stored or moved their laboratories while they acquired additional chemicals. One of the strategies that American law enforcement officials adopted was to try to make it difficult for laboratories to get their hands on the necessary chemicals for speed production. The harder it became to obtain the precursor chemicals, the more resourceful and ingenious the drug producers had to become. In an attempt to evade detection, illicit drug manufacturers sometimes had to cross vast distances to acquire chemicals and equipment. They would scour the land for suitable substances. No possibilities were ruled out – not even stealing fertilizers from farmers. The American Corn Belt swims with nitrogen fertilizer, which can double as one of the components in the manufacture of speed. The Corn Belt uses more of this chemically volatile substance than any other region in the country and the isolated farmhouses and storage sheds of the Midwest provided rich and easy pickings for speed producers.

Clandestine laboratory operators were also frequently well-armed. They were, after all, the other side in the "war on drugs". Their laboratories had to be guarded and protected both from the law and from rival producers. They were always ready for any eventuality; weapons, including explosives, were routinely confiscated in police raids on laboratories. Operators usually disposed of their hazardous chemical waste unsafely and illegally, often dumping the waste on the ground, in nearby streams and lakes or just pouring it into the local sewerage system. The illicit manufacture of speed was based primarily in the west and south-west of the USA. In 1994, drug enforcement field divisions in Houston, Denver, Phoenix, St Louis, Los Angeles, San Diego, San Francisco and New Orleans accounted for over 86 per cent of the speed laboratory seizures nationwide.

TRACKING YOUR PREY

The US Department of Justice gradually began to target the biker groups. By the 1980s, a combination of law enforcement pressure and a shift to new methods of manufacture led to significant changes in the speed production/distribution network. The trend was towards smaller producers and groups of friends and family, who co-operated to produce limited amounts of the drug in low-tech labs. In the early 1980s, organized crime syndicates began to manufacture ephedrine-type speed in the eastern areas of San Diego County. Throughout the 1980s, young, working class whites took to this local, long-acting and inexpensive speed to such an extent that San Diego came to be known in the USA as "the Bogota of speed".

At first, the authorities paid very little attention to the increasing general production and use of this "poor man's cocaine", which quietly continued to spread across the nation. By the end of the 1980s, the

Federal Drug Enforcement Agency (FDEA), an agency within the Department of Justice, was having some success in the war against illicit producers. The number of laboratories seized rose dramatically during the 1980s from 88 in 1981 to 652 in 1989. This increase reflects both increased law enforcement and the rapid expansion of the illicit speed manufacturing trade. Since the late 1980s, there has been a decrease in the number of labs that have been discovered in the USA. In 1992, 332 clandestine laboratories were seized. The following year there were 270 seizures, with a further 306 seizures in 1994. This is believed to be largely as a result of the enactment and enforcement of a law that placed the 12 precursors and eight essential chemicals used in the production of illicit speed under federal control. Today, the FDEA reports that speed is now the most prevalent illicitly manufactured, controlled substance in the USA and has been so for the past twenty years, since around 1979.

THE EPHEDRINE LINK

Currently, the ephedrine reduction method is the principal means employed in the manufacture of methamphetamine in the USA. This relatively simple process originated in southern California and is now widespread throughout the United States. The process results

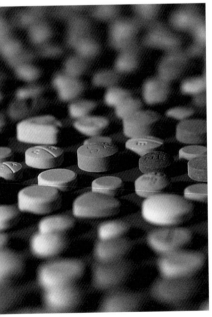

in a final product known as d-methamphetamine hydrochloride. Prior to the popularity of the ephedrine reduction method, the most common method for making methamphetamine was the phenyl-2-propanone (P2P) process. This method produces a racemic mixture known as dl-methamphetamine hydrochloride.

Some laboratory operators continued to use the P2P method for a while. But by the latter half of 1994, clandestine laboratory operators shifted noticeably from ephedrine tablets to pseudo-ephedrine tablets as their source of ephedrine. This coincided with the placing of stronger controls on single-entity ephedrine tablets and the elimination of the threshold for ephedrine transactions. In the meantime, the FDEA opened or continued investigations into rogue ephedrine and pseudo-ephedrine tablet manufacturers and mail order distributors located in the eastern USA. These suppliers diverted

SPEED TABLETS

millions of tablets to customers in California and other western states for delivery to illicit speed manufacturing laboratories.

THE "BIG HITTERS"

The FDEA believes there is now a new and more serious domestic threat regarding speed production, trafficking and distribution, particularly in the western states of the USA. Their main concern is over the involvement of Mexican poly-drug organizations that, over the past few years, have replaced the outlaw motorcycle gangs as the predominant speed producers, traffickers and distributors in California and much of the western United States. Having significantly expanded their production capacity, the Mexican organizations have virtually saturated the western US market with high-purity speed. By contrast, fifteen years earlier, the manufacture of speed was still a cottage industry with laboratories set up primarily in homes or in small-scale outfits. The Mexicans are much better organized, better funded, better equipped and much more serious about their occupation and the extraordinary profits they can make than the biker gangs or small producers ever were. These organizations are willing to pay the going rate for the precursor chemicals they need. They routinely pay $10,000 or more in cash for the diverted ephedrine and pseudo-ephedrine tablets and use multiple names and addresses to conduct their illicit transactions.

ASIAN ICE

Prior to 1990, all the ice coming into Hawaii originated from Far East Asian sources, especially in the Philippines, Korea, Taiwan and Japan. Ice distribution in Hawaii was an economic enterprise developed by well-organized crime networks in Japan and Korea with large corporate investors. Manufacturing began in the Far East where there is a free flow of ephedrine – the essential precursor for the making of ice – as the ephedra plant grows naturally in that part of the world. Some reports indicate that Korean manufacturers may have been the first to begin large-scale production in the early 1980s. They then transferred their bases either to Taiwan or the Philippines after heavy pressure from Korean law enforcement agencies. According to law enforcement and street sources in Hawaii, there seems to be a particular link between the Koreans and Filipinos. One street source spoken to in a Hawaiian drugs study, put it this way:

"Most people don't know what is really happening. Most people think it's the Filipinos in control – but the Koreans give 'em to the Filipinos 'cause the Filipinos don't talk too much... the Filipinos keep their mouth shut! The Koreans don't get into the labour part, they won't take risks, they just play the big man and distribute. The Filipinos do

the dirty work. The stuff comes from Korea, so the only way they can get it is from Koreans."

Although opinion is generally agreed that most ice is manufactured and distributed from the Far East, opinion varies widely about the exact sources and distribution routes. In the autumn of 1993, a speed laboratory capable of producing large quantities of ice was discovered in Taiwan. Police seized over 400kg of the semi-finished product, which would have yielded over 200kg of ice. Analysis revealed that most of the drug manufactured at the laboratory was being shipped to Japan and South Korea. Other intelligence sources also indicate that ice for the international market continued – and still continues – to be produced in the Guangdong Province of China.

One consequence of the ice "gold-rush" era in Hawaii has been that individuals got on the dealing bandwagon and developed alternative sources. Hawaiians started making trips to the US West Coast, buying methamphetamine at mainland prices, bringing it back and attempting to turn it into ice for a small profit. Consequently, fly-by-night dealer networks sprang up, resulting in a saturated market and virtually no quality control at all. More recent, well-documented evidence suggests the existence of ice networks involving mainland USA, Canada and Mexico. The first known operational ice laboratory in southern California was seized in Los Angeles in September 1993.

SWITCHING TO EUROPE

While the last decade has seen a steady decline in the number of speed laboratories detected in the USA and the Far East, during the same period, the amount of speed originating from western Europe has doubled and eastern Europe's share of the global market has also risen sharply, from zero to 12 per cent. As a result, Europe has become the major global centre of illicit speed production and use. In the 1991–94 period, Europe accounted for 64 per cent of all speed detections world-wide. Most laboratories have been detected in the UK, Netherlands and Germany. According to Interpol, the main European sources for speed used to be the Netherlands – many European countries have reported that 70 to 80 per cent of their illicitly imported amphetamine originated there – followed by Belgium, Denmark, Germany, Spain and the UK.

From 1984–1994, the number of seizures made in the UK rose sharply from under three thousand to nearly thirteen thousand with the biggest increase coming in the period since 1992. Over the same time-span, the actual amount of speed seized jumped from 59kg to over 1,300kg and, once again, the biggest increases have been since 1992. In 1994, as a percentage of all seizures, those for speed ranked second only behind cannabis. A majority of countries in western Europe, including France, Switzerland, Germany, UK, Spain and the Nordic countries, as well as a majority of countries in eastern Europe, saw rising levels of speed use during the 1990s. In fact, in the mid 1990s, the biggest increase in the use of speed globally was reported from Europe.

THE UK PERSPECTIVE

The history of speed distribution in the UK has never been fully investigated. In the early days, most of the speed in circulation around the clubs was in the form of pharmaceutically manufactured pills. As these pills invariably had the manufacturer's initials, SKF, stamped on them, those working with chronic speed users in Soho came to the conclusion that vast quantities of drugs were finding their way directly to the dealers via Smith, Kline and French employees. Some employees helped local "families" remove hundreds of thousands of pills from the main factory or from large warehouses in and around the London area. The SKF factory was based in Welwyn Garden City, not far from London, so vast quantities of speed pills could be moved on to the streets very easily. At a meeting of the Society for the Study of Addiction in September, 1966, one worker, Judith Piepe, drew the society's attention to the problem:

"We know what is happening. Extensive security precautions in a factory cost a great deal of money. It is quite easy for anybody on the production line to quietly take some pills and augment their wages by selling them. The production cost of drugs like Drinamyl are very low and the cost in money to ensure better security arrangements are considered too high by the manufacturers. But they do not consider the cost in suffering to young people."

At about this time, the press reported a Gloucestershire doctor as saying that he knew that speed was being made by teenagers with O-level chemistry. He offered no evidence for this and the *Daily Mirror* rang various experts to check the story. One GP, Ian Pierce James, stated he was sure that anyone with O-level chemistry could make speed pills, but he wasn't sure how they managed to make the little moulds with the SKF stamp on them! In March 1967, an article in the underground magazine Oz reported on two 21-year-old dealers, Paul and Cliff:

"Starting their work at the Marquee club, they sell to a market of 13-year-old mods; after a meal they move into the clubs around Greek Street; then to a stand just outside Tiffany's at about one in the morning. When necessary, they work a pitch at the Lyon's Cafés around Trafalgar Square; if one Sunday morning they have any pills remaining, they move into Chelsea where apparently tired debs are always a ready market."

So who exactly were the main people involved? At the top may have sat members of Britain's most notorious criminal gangs of the 1960s. They owned many of London's West End clubs and would have been unlikely to allow any profitable side action to be carried out on their "patch" without ensuring a cut for themselves. Also, there was a marked increase in the incidence of break-ins at pharmacies all over the country. As most pharmacies at this time did not have a secure drugs cabinet, it was easy to steal speed in bulk. It was a simple matter of breaking into a pharmacy, taking the bottles off a shelf and walking out. A burglar could come away with over ten thousand pills in a single raid on a pharmacy. In 1968, there were thirty cases of theft from pharmacies reported in the Nottingham area alone.

For decades, speed users were lucky enough to get pharmaceutical grade products, made for the medical profession and for sale over the counter. The purity of the contents was never an issue. But once speed use began to be fairly widespread, controlling legislation was brought in and the availability of the drug was drastically reduced. Like any other drug that has been available in sufficient quantities to create a demand and then withdrawn, alternative sources of supply were soon developed.

Once the curb on prescriptions began to take effect, several teams of enterprising young manufacturers all over the UK began to make speed. Amphetamine sulphate is the easiest form of speed to produce. With a little ingenuity and some chemistry knowledge, anyone could go into the speed business. The base materials are available even today, using chemicals that, with some difficulty, can still be purchased in the UK.

Copying their counterparts in the USA, manufacturers would rent space in industrial estates or use buildings in isolated parts of the country. Many of the laboratories raided in the 1970s and 1980s were located in factory sites and remote areas in and around Essex, Norfolk, Suffolk and the Midlands. Here they would set up laboratories for just three or four months at a time, producing vast quantities of speed for the street. If informants warned them that they had been discovered, they would abandon all their equipment and flee. They did not need to worry about the loss of the laboratory as it had not cost much to set up in the first place and their profits easily covered the outlay.

LONG ARM OF THE LAW

It is a moot point why some drugs are prohibited while others are licensed for sale. Even the basis for the legal distinctions between licit and illicit recreational drugs are hard to justify. These distinctions cannot possibly be based on a calculation of risk or social disruption, since nobody could possibly doubt the toxicity of tobacco smoke or the personal and public harm associated with the excessive use of alcohol. Nor can these distinctions relate to the addictive potential of these drugs, since nicotine is one of the most addictive of all drugs and tranquillizers are still being prescribed in large numbers. Neither can it be because of a taboo against intoxication or loss of personal control – as there are very few situations more intimidating or depressing than witnessing a pack of drunks reeling toward you along a city street at night, urinating against walls, smashing windows and howling obscenities. Drug addicts presenting to the average GP or drug-dependency clinic are no more representative of general drug use in society than skid-row alcoholics are of ordinary social drinking.

In Victorian times, only a century or so ago, the drug scene in the West was very different from that of today. Large sectors of the population consumed opiate drugs, cocaine and marijuana provided by a patent-medicine industry run by a handful of men, who became exceedingly rich on the profits. And it was all legitimate. Drugs now feared and reviled were respectable entries in the medical pharmacopoeias of the time. In the UK, far from using the might of the military to keep drugs out of the country, the Royal Navy helped protect British exports of opium to China. In fact, Britain was the most powerful international drug trafficker of the age, not only fighting the Chinese to protect their market, but also combating mounting outside pressure to end the trade. Suffice it to say that international politics, rather than medical harm-reduction, has played a great part in the evolution of drugs law enforcement.

The regulation of illicit drugs in most countries during the twentieth century has centred around three basic aims: to prohibit, or at least reduce, the supply of illicit drugs, to stifle the demand for them and to provide treatment for those who develop drug-related problems. Global drug prohibition currently involves the suppression, by force, of any unauthorized manufacture, trafficking across national frontiers, marketing, and personal use of illicit substances. This is today's "war on drugs". To this end, governments usually start by strengthening their drug laws and then expanding their police, customs, judicial and probation services in order to enforce it. Sooner or later, the long arm of the law descends heavily on the manufacturers and traffickers and often mercilessly on the end-users of any illicit drug. Some governments establish considerably more draconian laws than others, no doubt influenced by the social acceptability or otherwise of drug use in their countries.

US DRUG LAWS

Since the enactment of the Harrison Narcotics Act in 1914, the USA has been at the forefront in the shaping of a global anti-drugs agenda. International policy making in this area is a relatively new process, not even a century old. Under American instigation, international treaties have theoretically obliged nations to combat drug use in their own countries. The first drugs to be tackled internationally were the "exotic" drugs. These drugs were largely derived from plants that occurred naturally in the southern hemisphere and had acquired reputations of great danger and by the early part of the twentieth century had been demonized by Western society. The dangerous nature of these drugs seemed to be enhanced by their foreign origins and their connections with Shamanism and non-Christian rites and rituals.

For decades, American-influenced international agencies have been hard at work in third-world producer countries, attempting to channel their traditional agricultural activities away from drug production. Only very much later on did international drug regulators turn their attention to synthetic chemicals being produced in vast pharmaceutical laboratories in the USA and Europe. In 1970, Public Law number 91-513, known as the Controlled Substances Act (CSA) was enacted. This law gave the Federal Drug Enforcement Agency power to supervise every person who legally handled controlled substances, including about 500,000 physicians, pharmacists, scientists and pharmaceutical drug manufacturers. Soon after the CSA became law, a comprehensive series of regulations was issued by the former Bureau of Narcotics and Dangerous Drugs. These regulations have been amended hundreds of times as new and different procedures, substances and exceptions to the rules appear.

The FDEA is responsible for enforcement and regulation of the CSA. Its purpose is to prevent the illegal use of controlled substances and ensure their use only by legally registered handlers. The US Government has issued the Controlled Substances Handbook for licensed handlers of abusable substances. This handbook contains all the rules and regulations for the proper handling of drugs of abuse. It also contains the various drug schedules.

When the CSA Handbook was first released, speed and its related drugs were placed in the Schedule III category. This category dealt with drugs that could lead to moderate or low addiction. With the rise in speed prescription and the widespread illicit use of the drug, however, the American agencies decided that something needed to be done to curb the trend. In 1971, with the support of the American Medical Association, these drugs were moved to the more stringent Schedule II category. In 1978, the Council on Scientific Affairs issued the following statement:

"When administering drugs of the amphetamine type for any medical reason...the physician should weigh their therapeutic efficacy against the disadvantages of abuse. The physician should be especially alert to aspects of the patient's current and past behaviour

that indicate risk of substance abuse or addiction. Dosages should be set as low as possible, the duration of therapy kept as short as possible, and drug holidays provided as often as possible. There is always the chance that the efficacy of a stimulant in helping a patient achieve a therapeutic goal may predispose him to look upon amphetamine-type drugs as desirable rather than hazardous substances, and open the door for future drug abuse."

Following the introduction of drug schedules and their subsequent enforcement, there was a decline in the amount of legally manufactured speed and its related compounds available. The direct impact that scheduling had on speed use, however, will never be fully known because so many other changes occurred at the same time. An increase in drug education, free evaluation and treatment services and information hotlines as well as improved law enforcement and increased penalties have all contributed to the decline in speed production and use.

Drug schedules provided the legal basis for the arrest of any unlicensed person for possession, use, and distribution of drugs. Physicians had to register with the FDEA in order to write a prescription for a controlled substance. For doctors, this meant a lot of paperwork and the need for special security systems, both of which contributed to a decrease in the number of prescriptions written for speed. Once speed was scheduled, the door was opened for a very profitable illicit speed market.

UK DRUG LAWS

The response to the speed problem by the UK establishment was heavily influenced by a model of drug use based on opium and, subsequently, heroin, and by the "British System" of treatment set up by the Rolleston Committee in the 1920s. The committee consisted of eminent physicians as addiction at that time was regarded primarily as a medical problem and so treatment was left to the clinical judgement of medical practitioners. Measures such as the official notification of addicts and compulsory treatment were both resisted. The UK's 1920 Dangerous Drugs Act differed very much from its American counterpart, the Harrison Act of 1914, in allowing medical practitioners considerable freedom in dealing with drug use and users. In the USA, by contrast, the addict was criminalized.

Speed has been prescribed in the UK to treat medical conditions since the 1920s. However, its use became increasingly popular among groups seeking the stimulant effect rather than needing treatment for a psychological or physical disorder, particularly when mixed with barbiturates, a combination known colloquially as "purple hearts". These social groups saw speed as attractive, as a recreational mood

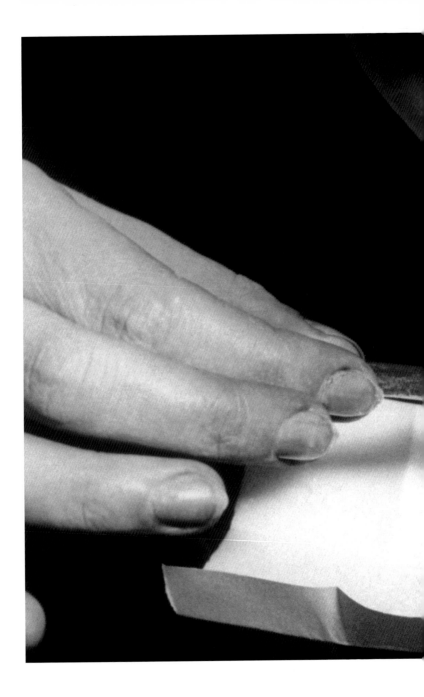

SPEED POWDER PREPARED FOR SNORTING

enhancer and as an instrument in which periods of recreation could be extended for hours on end without any need for sleep.

The first reference to the adverse effects of speed appeared in the *Pharmaceutical Journal* of June 1936, quoting a report that the drug produced hypertension (high blood pressure). In the same journal, in May 1937, there appeared a comment on references in the daily newspapers to the non-therapeutic use of Benzedrine by the general public. By that time, one major company of multiple chemists had already decided to supply the drug to the general public only on prescription, even though the law at that time allowed for the free sale of speed. In June 1939, the UK Government placed Benzedrine on Part 1 of the Poisons List with the proviso that the drug should be labelled: *"Caution – it is dangerous to take this preparation except under medical supervision."*

By 1954, the demand for speed had increased and pharmacists were responding to the demand for its provision by stocking up. It was at this time that reports appeared of the non-therapeutic use of nasal amphetamine inhalers. Speed and its compounds were placed in Schedule IV of the Poisons Rule and could only be obtained on prescription, except for preparations in an inhaler. This only served to encourage increased non-therapeutic use and the manufacturers responded either by withdrawing their products from the market or by altering the formulation.

The casual use of speed was not the only cause for concern. In 1958, a monograph on amphetamine psychosis was published, which described a drug-induced mental condition that mimicked schizophrenia. The author reported that this could occur with low doses of speed in some patients. In the following years, mounting concern over the increasing non-medical use by young persons of drugs containing speed, either alone or in combination with barbiturates, became a matter for debate in the Houses of Parliament and in the British press. At the same time, the police became aware of the widespread use of these drugs and the customs authorities were gathering evidence that speed was also being imported into the country.

The Drugs (Prevention of Misuse) Act was introduced in March 1964. It then became illegal to be in unauthorized possession of drugs of the amphetamine type or to import them without a licence. Amphetamines, being Class B controlled drugs, are now only legally obtainable on prescription in the UK. This means they can only be supplied by a pharmacist working from a registered pharmacy on presentation of a doctor's prescription. Patients can legitimately possess them on prescription, but otherwise their unauthorized production, supply or possession is an offence. It is also an offence to allow premises to be used for producing or supplying or using speed. All the different types of speed are controlled under Class B of the Act – but if any of them are prepared for injection, they also fall under the increased penalties of Class A controlled drugs (which also includes cocaine and heroin).

A GLOBAL APPROACH

The World Health Organization (WHO) became aware of the problem of speed in the early 1950s. The United Nations Expert Committee that met in 1952 was concerned with its use by intravenous opiate users, who were injecting speed when opiates were not available. In conclusion, it recommended that a close watch be kept on the use of speed internationally. The following year, the Expert Committee discussed the subject again and recommended that governments should take measures to strengthen the controls on speed at a national level. The control measures that the committee recommended were over the prescription of the drug: speed should only be dispensed on prescription, each prescription should specify the number of refills and a careful record should be kept of all prescriptions written. Even by 1956, the WHO considered that it was a local problem only that could be tackled swiftly by each nation taking individual measures and was not an issue that warranted international action. This perception slowly changed during the following decade as an increasing number of countries, including Sweden, Japan, the USA, the UK and Australia began to face serious problems.

By the early 1960s, there came into existence the Single Convention on Narcotic Drugs (1961). This convention controlled opium, opiates and synthetic opioids, as well as coca leaves, cannabis and all their derivatives. But this convention did not cover speed. By the mid 1960s, there began discussions at the UN Commission on Narcotic Drugs on the desirability of setting up an international system of control for all psychotropic substances. The UN Expert Committee, held in 1969, contributed to this discussion by presenting a draft protocol on psychotropic substances together with proposed lists of CNS stimulants, depressants and hallucinogens that were to be placed under control.

Most of those proposals were accepted by the United Nations and incorporated into the Convention on Psychotropic Substances adopted in 1971. The list of 32 substances placed under international control now included speed. Since the time the Convention came into effect in 1976, the number of controlled substances has increased from 32 to 105. The procedure for modifying the list involves a medical and scientific assessment by the WHO and a final decision by the United Nations.

The signatory nations to the Single Convention on Narcotic Drugs and the Convention on Psychotropic Substances are required "to limit to *medical* and scientific purposes the cultivation, production, manufacture, export, import, distribution of, trade in, use and possession of [certain] drugs." Draconian methods for the enforcement of these controls are justified by the grave public health, social and economic risks that drugs are said to pose to society. A licensing system enables the International Narcotics Control Board to monitor the worldwide trade in illicit drugs.

COPING WITH AN "EPIDEMIC"

A drugs "problem" can often by handled by the various agencies responsible in society – but a drug "epidemic" is a different matter altogether. Not many countries have experienced speed epidemics – Sweden and Japan are two notable exceptions. Although very different in many respects, these two countries have in common the fact that the illicit use of amphetamine is deeply ingrained in their societies. Unlike other nations, which have experienced severe problems with a range of different drugs, in Japan and Sweden amphetamine and methamphetamine have remained the drugs of choice. These two countries are similar in other ways too. They have both developed legislation and initiated law enforcement policies that are particularly severe. Both would claim that these measures have resulted in some containment of the problem and both attribute a considerable proportion of their difficulties to the policies, or lack of them, of neighbouring countries.

It is interesting to place them in close juxtaposition, not only to highlight similarities, but to note the differences between them in their cultures; their political, military and economic history, and their attitudes and experiences of other drugs. It may be that if the use of amphetamine by Japan and Sweden were better understood, it would throw some light on the patterns of use observed elsewhere in the world.

WIDE-EYED IN TOKYO

During World War II, methamphetamine was given mainly to help achieve Japanese military objectives. At times, soldiers were forced to consume speed to enhance their fighting spirits. In 1941, pharmacies began to sell speed over the counter under brand names such as Philopon and Sedrin. However, speed abuse was not a social issue in Japan at that time. Japan was a totalitarian society, led by a powerful military regime, in which the people shared the same objectives as their leaders. Under such circumstances, people did not think of speed use in terms of potential harm or drug dependence. Most Japanese were completely ignorant of the potentially hazardous properties of speed and no laws controlling its sale or distribution existed at this time.

JAPAN EXPERIENCED THE WORLD'S FIRST SPEED EPIDEMIC

By the end of the war in 1945, there were vast stockpiles of speed left all around the world. These stores of drugs, previously held by the Japanese military, were now sold on the black market in many countries. In Japan, the production of speed had been increased to maximum capacity during the war. Now that the war was over, there was no longer a need for speed to prop up the Imperial war effort. Over-zealous and misguided pharmaceutical companies dumped large quantities of hoarded speed on to the open civilian market. This flooding of the black market led to widespread use among the civilian population in Japan. The excess supplied over a million chronic users and several million less regular users. Allied with its availability was the incredibly affordable nature of speed. This allowed people to develop a "taste" for the drug and to actually maintain that taste. A vigorous advertising campaign by the pharmaceutical companies promoted this stimulating drug as "Wakemine" with slogans such as "Fight sleepiness and enhance vitality". These advertisements claimed that speed could help individuals cope with the devastation and the severe hardships caused by the social, cultural and industrial upheavals of the post-war period. Speed use spread rapidly in a society that was discouraged and depressed by the outcome of the war. The younger generation, especially, was eager to experience the euphoric and mood-elevating effects of speed. Writers, journalists, artists, entertainers, students and even factory workers were using speed to enhance their efficacy and to make themselves feel better. Speed may have seemed to be helping alleviate tensions and hardship, but it soon brought home the lesson that you can have too much of a good thing.

The three main social factors: an aimless, nihilistic and confused post-war social environment; an unlimited supply of speed in the marketplace and the demands of the younger generation for the euphoric effects of speed brought about the world's first speed epidemic or "street craze". At the height of the epidemic, in 1954, it was estimated that over two million of Japan's population of 88.5 million people had become habitual users of speed.

The Japanese state felt it had no choice but to respond with severe measures to tackle the situation. The attack was two pronged: prevention and cure. Education and treatment programmes began in 1954. Legal changes quickly followed and cut straight into the supply chain. Once the penalties for sale and use were increased, the grip of the speed epidemic was weakened. The police crackdown on the illicit market in Japan was swift and successful with sweeping arrests and stiff prison sentences. In a little over a year, by the end of 1955, the casual use of speed had been sharply controlled.

SWEDEN

Sweden is one of the three most recent members of the European Community, joining in 1995. Located on the Scandinavian peninsula, Sweden is the fourth largest country in Europe but has a population of only 8.5 million people, with the highest density in the south of the country. The capital, Stockholm, is the largest city with just above 1.5 million inhabitants. Sweden has vast resources of iron ore and timber, and mining, steel and forest industries form the basis of the economy. Thanks to its geographical location, a policy of non-alignment in peace, neutrality in war and a great deal of luck, Sweden was able to stay out of both world wars, with subsequent economic advantages resulting in rapid economic growth, particularly after 1945.

The population of Sweden is relatively homogenous in language, ethnic stock and religion (although Swedes in general are not very religious). All Swedish citizens are registered with a personal identity code, which facilitates government administration and makes it easier to gather reliable statistical information about the population, but also leads to concerns about the infringement of civil liberties.

Speed was introduced in Sweden by Prinzmetal and Bloomberg in 1935, shortly after it first became available in general clinical practice, and it was sold without prescription until 1939. Sweden had a serious post-war drug problem far earlier than other European countries and the main drugs of abuse were speed and its related substances. The first reports of abuse appeared in 1944 and, in the same year, speed was incorporated under existing legislation on narcotic drugs in Sweden. Due to the relative prosperity in Sweden after the Second

World War, when the rest of Europe was underfed or even starving, it was the only country where obesity was a health problem in the general population. This may have been one reason why speed, at this time often used for weight reduction, was more abundant in Sweden than in other European countries.

Toward the end of the 1940s, a new form of illicit amphetamine emerged in Stockholm, centred around a narrow clique of "bohemians" including authors, musicians and artists. Some of these new users were heavy drinkers who initially took speed as a hangover cure but later switched from alcohol to speed as their drug of choice. Until this time, only oral abuse of speed was reported, but one of the central figures of the artistic clique, a well-known poet of the time, has reported that he first injected amphetamine in 1949. This bohemian core of speed users probably consisted of no more than a few dozen people at the time, but drug use soon spread to criminally active youth in Stockholm. By the early 1950s, field social workers in Stockholm began to be concerned about the widespread use of speed among young people. By 1954, when the first prison sentence for illicit dealing in stimulants was handed down by a Swedish court, drug peddling had become quite extensive.

The bulk of the drugs being used still originated from prescriptions issued by unsuspecting doctors and this was acknowledged by the Swedish National Board of Health in a statement in 1960. According to the Board, drug users preferentially turned to older doctors, often retired from medical practice, sometimes living in the countryside, and very often only a telephone call was needed to obtain a prescription. But the board didn't impose any restrictions. They simply criticized doctors for issuing prescriptions without checking the identity of their patients. It wasn't until 1962 that the Board imposed restrictions on the prescribing by telephone of narcotic drugs (maximum of five tablets and no preparations for injecting). This put a stop to one source, but the street market had already been established and by now there were other channels in place.

A debate about government strategy on drugs was initiated in 1964. The traditionally restrictive policy was questioned and a more liberal policy was advocated. Following a large media campaign in favour of a liberalization of drug policy, an experimental plan was initiated in 1965 to allow stimulants and opiates for injection to be prescribed legally. It was hoped that this would avoid drug users having to commit crime to acquire the drugs they needed. The drugs were to be prescribed in decreasing doses so that users would slowly be weaned off their addiction.

The experiment didn't work for several reasons. Many of the users were already criminals before they even started taking drugs and their criminal

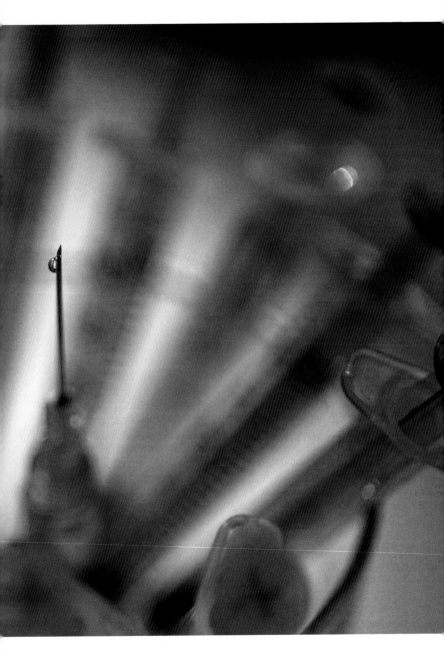

INJECTING SPEED USERS ARE NOT ALWAYS AWARE OF THE HEALTH RISKS

nature was not changed by the fact that they were now getting their drugs on prescription. Furthermore, the idea of curing addiction by giving decreasing doses of a drug was borrowed from a heroin detoxification programme, which didn't work for stimulants. Most importantly, the experiment did not take into account the epidemic nature of speed use in Stockholm and how contagious this epidemic was. The experiment was eventually stopped in May 1967, mainly in response to the death of a young girl from an overdose of morphine and speed, legally prescribed to another person.

The failure of this experiment thoroughly discredited the policy of legalizing the distribution of narcotic drugs to users for a very long time. In the following years, debate focused on the battle against illicit drugs. The Narcotic Drugs Act came into force in 1968 and was based on the international conventions that Sweden has ratified. It has been amended several times toward greater restrictions and an emphasis on prevention.

According to information from experienced drugs users in Sweden, not only the use but also the import and trade in speed is dominated by native Swedes today. The main import routes for speed are from the Netherlands, Poland and increasingly from parts of the former Soviet Union. The purity of speed on the street is about 8–10 per cent. Dutch speed is better quality and can cost up to 300 Swedish Crowns per gram compared to around 1000 SC for heroin. Among injecting users, methamphetamine is still the most popular drug of choice, although heroin has slowly gained ground.

Sweden's entry into the European Community, now that the customs officials can no longer make such rigorous checks at the border, is feared to lead to an increase in the illegal importation of drugs into the country. With increased integration within Europe may also come new influences on existing national drug patterns as well as on policy makers.

EUROPEAN DILEMMAS

Currently, there is a new drug liberalization movement in Europe. In November 1990, the cities of Amsterdam, Frankfurt am Main, Hamburg and Zurich issued a document named "European Cities on Drug Policy", the so-called Frankfurt Resolution. This resolution states that drug problems in society are primarily due to the illegality of drug consumption, which makes drugs impure and expensive and causes misery, death and "acquisitive criminality". Consequently, the resolution proposes, among other things, the provision of "shooting galleries" in which drugs can be consumed under supervision and that "medically controlled prescriptions of drugs to long-term users should be analysed without prejudice and in view of harm reduction". Some 23 cities and municipalities in Europe have now adopted this resolution.

The first serious opposition to the Frankfurt Resolution came at a meeting held in Stockholm, in April 1994, with the issuing of a document entitled "European Cities Against Drugs", the so-called Stockholm Resolution. In this resolution, all proposals to legalize illicit drugs are rejected and a restrictive drugs policy based on the international drugs conventions adopted by the UN is advocated. So far, 21 cities, among them Paris, Berlin and London and several other capitals, have adopted the Stockholm Resolution.

EDUCATION OR MISINFORMATION?

The same dilemma over finding an effective drugs policy that grips the European governments is also faced by those who deal with the issue of drugs education. When it comes to the question of what to teach children about drugs and their effects, many parents and teachers believe it is best to avoid telling the whole truth. Over decades, the broad education policy has simply been an extension of the "war on drugs" policy. Children are told that all drugs are equally bad for them and can kill – with no distinction made between different drugs. When children are taught about drugs in this general, blanket way – they inevitably become confused and many, being children, are attracted to the forbidden. One 14-year-old, interviewed about drug use for a television programme, explained how she had developed a chronic crack habit:

"All they told us at school was that all drugs were bad for us and that we should stay away from them. The examples they would use to put us off drugs were the rock stars! What the teachers didn't realize was that these people are glamorous to us kids and we couldn't wait to be like them. I started by smoking joints with my friends. I was shocked. It was nothing like the teachers had told us – it didn't make me sick and nor did it kill me. I actually quite enjoyed it. A year or so after I had been smoking weed, I was given some crack to try and smoke. I thought it would just be a better hit than the weed and so I did it. I did it a few more times with my friends and before I knew it I was hooked. If my teachers had told me the truth about different drugs, I think I would have known where to draw the line."

Although young people are also warned at school about the severe criminal penalties for drug use, many of them will experiment with drugs and many of these will become habitual users. Peer pressure plays a large part in the reason why young people try drugs. Many of them want to look "cool" and not lose face in front of friends.

One country in Europe that takes a different approach to drugs education is the Netherlands. As with their sex education, the Dutch authorities believe in being as open as possible with their students. Young people are taught about different drugs, their short- and long-term effects, and where to find help if they get into trouble. Another important element of Netherlands' drugs policy is that young people who want to try drugs, "just to see what they are like", can go into a coffee shop and use marijuana without breaking the law. There is a belief that once a young person is able to try an illicit substance, he or she will quite often lose interest in it. Consequently, the Netherlands has a relatively minor drugs problem among its young people compared with other parts of Europe.

THE HIV CONNECTION

The profile of the typical speed user in the USA would be: heterosexual, sexually active, employed, well-integrated into society, and well able to interact socially and sexually with the non drug-using population. A significant number of speed users in the USA are intravenous injectors, however, and this is a cause of some alarm among drugs workers and health workers alike. In addition to the direct effects of the drug and legal penalties for speed use, injectors have a much greater risk of acquiring HIV, hepatitis and other bloodborne viral infections.

In California, it is estimated that there are around seven thousand people who inject speed daily, and an unknown number of occasional injectors. Yet, in comparison to heroin or cocaine or crack, speed has a low profile in drugs awareness programmes and there has been a lack of provision of any form of substitution therapy. As a result, speed users find it very difficult to present themselves to local needle exchange or drug treatment programmes. They feel that they do not get treated the same way as those hooked on heroin, for example. Because of this reluctance, speed injectors continue to use old drug equipment, such as needles and syringes, leaving them vulnerable to a wide range of serious infections.

While the incidence of HIV among injecting drug users in California is quite high, it is not possible to say for sure that the drug equipment used was the source of infection or whether there was another cause. It is not only the injecting of speed that poses a serious threat to health, the sexual behaviour of some speed injectors also increases the risk of acquiring and transmitting HIV. Many speed injectors have numerous sexual partners during the course of a year and very few of them bother to wear a condom during intercourse. What is becoming obvious, through various studies undertaken, is that injecting users have very little time for their general health, and will indulge in unhealthy and unsafe behaviour when under the influence of their drug.

Alternative avenues of treatment and help need to be found for intravenous speed users who are not responding to the current services available for drug addicts. Harm-reduction strategies have to be re-thought and restructured to accommodate speed users. Given the increasing popularity of speed as a drug of choice, especially among young people, target-specific drugs education and health advice is crucial. A non-judgmental needle-exchange, where the user is simply given clean equipment, along with advice on safer sex and some free condoms, can go a long way toward alleviating the problem, as many projects in Amsterdam have shown. Peer pressure can also be brought to bear to help change unsafe behaviour. One of the most effective methods has been street outreach. With street outreach, workers are indigenous to the area and familiar with the people and the various sub-cultures that exist within the speed-using community. A local outreach worker often has enough influence to persuade those most at risk to steer clear of practices that can lead to HIV infection.

DEMAND AND SUPPLY

It is a rule of any market that demand and supply go hand-in-hand. A producer can artificially increase desire for a product, but that desire cannot be sustained for long as just a slogan stuck on to large drug stockpiles. Drug use is increasing because people want to consume and, in turn, suppliers have succeeded in accommodating their particular appetites. Like the pharmaceutical business, the trade in illicit drugs is a global commercial enterprise, yet it is much more complex and dynamic because it must constantly outwit a vast enforcement effort attempting to beat it into submission.

There are few other areas of crime where so many different laws are broken on a regular basis. False names, forged passports, phoney driving licences, money laundering, tax evasion, customs dodging, stolen vehicles, illegal planes, false documents. You name it – a drug manufacturer or trafficker has broken it. Drug profits have always been able to dazzle the dealers, from small-time back-alley pushers to the mightiest international drug barons. Some have said that the pull of drug money is sometimes stronger than the pull of the drug itself.

One story from the recent past illustrates the scale of the illicit drug business. In 1985, a trafficker was sentenced to fifty years imprisonment in Florida. In his six years of dealing, he had sold nearly 700,000kg (1.5 million lb) of Colombian marijuana, amassing in the process a phenomenal personal fortune of $750 million. The problem for him was that he could not find a bank that could "launder" such a huge amount – so he bought one!

THE DEVIL'S REAL NAME

The statistics of today's drug scene are both mind-boggling and quite meaningless. Nobody really knows how many people use any particular illicit drug, what the illicit drug market is worth or how much of it is seized by police and customs. Millions of dollars of government money chase a business worth billions, which in turn supplies the drug needs and demands of yet more unquantified millions. There is a saying that *"to know a devil's real name is to be his master"*, so too with drug statistics: a belief seems to exist in law enforcement circles that quantification – however piecemeal and inaccurate – puts them on the road to taming the beast. One speed statistic is rather interesting, though, and bears some looking at. For all the untold amount of speed taken through the 1960s and 1970s in the UK, there is not one case report of a speed-related club death recorded in any of the literature.

Today, in both the USA and UK, speed is the second most popular illicit drug after cannabis. That speed has re-emerged as the drug of choice for the younger generation of the 1990s is quite obvious. What cannot be said is that speed is the only drug being used. The drug culture of today is of a generation of people who are poly-drug users. They will experiment with almost anything. The choice of drug is based on one thing only – the size of their wallets. The young or student user without much money will still turn to cannabis and speed as the two prime drugs for those who want to have a good time on a restricted budget.

FRONT PAGE NEWS

Speed lacks the historical lineage and eloquent advocacy peculiar to cocaine or heroin. By and large it is a rough and ready drug, with a rough and ready clientele. Despite being second only to cannabis in prevalence, speed has attracted relatively little attention or coverage, in either the scientific literature or the popular media. Speed is often kept out of the limelight by the glare emanating from the aura of "evil" surrounding crack or junk.

Those who don't take illicit drugs are often afraid of those who do, and those who do take them are afraid of being exposed by society and punished by the law, which all adds to the climate of fear. All the time, the flames of this fear are being fanned by an ever-watchful media that is often ill informed, and also at times both hysterical and hypocritical. Drugs in our midst are, without exception, depicted as evil. Drug dealers are seen as the spawn of the devil, a menace that must be stamped out and drug users are portrayed either as sad, pathetic victims or as dangerous deviants.

DRUG SCANDALS

Drugs have been at the heart of many of the great scandals of the twentieth century. Drug-related stories, escapades or deaths are only scandalous because society makes them so. News consumers, with their voyeurism and insatiable appetite for moral outrage, collude with news producers to continue the long-standing tradition of hyperbole and sensationalism in news reporting. In this age of poly-drug use and increased confusion about how we handle drugs and their users, drug-related scandals have become a source of entertainment in their own right.

The media, it would seem, think that a good way to sell papers or increase ratings is by plastering stories of celebrities and drugs over their front pages with banner headlines and sensationalist language.

The public are also complicit in this game – it is their appetite for a spectacle that feeds the fires in the first place. The long highway to popular immortality is strewn with the wrecks of smashed cars and planes, while in the toilets and motel rooms lie the bodies of those who have taken a trip too far. A star dying from an overdose is the cherry on the cake for journalists looking for the ultimate drug story. Of all the "celebrity" drugs, speed has been an unmitigated disaster for the hacks. Unlike barbiturates, speed is not a drug that it is easy to overdose on and so not many people, let alone celebrities, have died specifically as a result of speed use.

BUSTED

As drug stories have provided great fodder for tabloid newspapers, some journalists haven't been backward in helping the stories happen. In 1967, the *News of the World* ran an article about a house in Roehampton rented by the Moody Blues and allegedly visited by musicians to sample drugs. Pete Townshend and Mick Jagger were among those named. An incensed Mick Jagger threatened to sue the paper, but the *News of the World* was not going to be put off so easily. A fortnight later, the newspaper carried a front page story headlined "Drug Squad Raids Pop Star's Party". No names or locations were mentioned on that first day. But the names were Mick Jagger and Keith Richard and the location was Redlands, Richard's house in West Sussex.

Following a tip off from the *News of the World*, nineteen local police officers turned up at Redlands armed with a search warrant. The house was searched and all the guests frisked. The police found some drugs, but missed a lot too. But the choicest find of all, and the one that justified the whole raid, incriminated Mick Jagger. A totemic figure, Jagger's face, according to Phillip Norman, was "engraved like a Wanted poster on so many policemen's minds". Jagger's jacket, a green velvet one, that he had last worn when holidaying on the French Riviera with Marianne Faithful just a few weeks earlier, was searched; inside was a small glass bottle containing four speed tablets, known as "black bombers". The tablets were actually Marianne's, but Jagger, ever the gent, immediately took the rap. The tablets were his, he said. He got them on prescription from his Harley Street doctor and used them *"to stay awake and work"*. The police left Redlands bearing their spoils.

The cases against Jagger and Richard were heard, Jagger was sentenced to three months and £200 costs and Richard was given a year in prison and £500 costs. The sentences of Jagger and Richard prompted the famous *Times* editorial of July 1, 1967: "Who Breaks a Butterfly on a Wheel?", claiming that the sentence imposed on Jagger reflected who he was rather than what he had done. Interestingly, Richard wasn't mentioned in this attack on social revenge, presumably because it would have diluted the argument. Jagger had only been involved with speed but Richard had been linked to cannabis smoking and was thus less morally defensible in the Britain of that time – a foreign herb as against a locally manufactured chemical that was still being prescribed by doctors. So it was rather ironic that, on appeal, Richard's conviction was quashed whereas Jagger's was left to stand, although the sentence was reduced to a conditional discharge.

POOR LITTLE RICH GIRLS

In the mid 1960s, the widespread use of speed pills and injectable Methedrine among New York's artistic community was creating a highly disturbed environment. Andy Warhol's "Factory" was the focal point for this frenetic East Coast sub-culture, where artists, poets, writers, musicians, models, groupies, sycophants and all sorts gathered in the desperate hope that Andy would give them their 15 minutes of fame.

Edie Sedgwick was Andy Warhol's superstar. She lived with Warhol and all his other hangers-on in The Factory. This young socialite turned actress lived a life of some spectacular success as Warhol's chosen one. She starred in many of the films he made at the Factory, including

Burn out baby – living fast and dying young

Kitchen, Vinyl, Beauty Part II and *Ciao, Manhattan*.

However fashionable they may have looked, a lot of the people hanging around at The Factory were volatile people, speeding like crazy to give themselves the confidence to "project an image". If Warhol was "the main man", then his trusted sidekick was Dr Charles Roberts. From his surgery, Dr Roberts dispensed shots of speed to whoever wanted them and had the money to pay for them. He shot up the entire cast of Warhol's movie, *Ciao, Manhattan*, with speed, in order to get the film finished more quickly!

On the recordings done for that film, Edie can be heard saying; *"Oh, that acrylic high, horrendous, yodelling, repetitious echoes of an infinity so brutally harrowing that words cannot capture the devastation nor the tone of such a vicious nightmare...[yet] it's hard to choose between the climactic ecstasies of speed and cocaine...oh, they are both so fabulous."*

All the time that she was there, Edie was ingesting every kind of drug she could get her hands on – but her favourite drug was speed. She would get her daily quota of speed from the junkie doctor, Roberts. As a fresh-faced and popular model, her pictures were in all the fashionable magazines from *Time Life* to *Vogue*. Her popularity reached a peak in the USA when Bob Dylan acknowledged that she had been the inspiration for his song *"Just Like a Woman"*.

By this time, Edie had a daily speed-injecting habit. This poor little rich girl was flying too high but no one at The Factory was in any fit state to notice that she was spiralling out of control. Edie died tragically young as a result of a lethal overdose of speed. But her mother put it a very different way – *"My girl died of neglect"*.

DEATH ON THE YELLOW BRICK ROAD

The same epitaph could be written for an even more famous star of screen and television, Judy Garland, the legendary singer and actress, and mother of Liza Minelli. Garland began taking speed pills to combat her weight. After the success and fame of her starring role as Dorothy in *The Wizard of Oz*, she began to increase the amount of speed she was taking. Inevitably, as time went on, she had to find something else to take the edge off and help her sleep. She turned to barbiturates. Soon, she was taking the two together and was caught up in a poly-drug habit that finally led to severe mental depression. A few stints in hospital and many attempted suicides later, Judy finally killed herself in a London loo.

Speed has always been a functional drug and there is no end to the various uses to which it can be put, or to the different kinds of people who find it useful. Professional jockeys have taken it to keep their weight down, as have cat-walk models to start with, before they moved on to

THE TRAGIC END OF A GLAMOROUS SCREEN ICON

the "cocaine and heroin chic" of today. Stage entertainers have found that it gave them the necessary zip for night after night of delivering the same lines or singing the same songs. In show business, studies show that those who achieve early success are more likely to become involved with stimulants. One reason given is that entertainers become so euphoric during a performance without drugs that when the show is over, they do not want to lose that feeling. They search for artificial ways to regain the "buzz" they gained from the applause and from being in the spotlight.

SPEED IN SPORT

The pressures exerted on people who work in the fields of sports and entertainment are very similar. Both professional athletes and entertainers are in the public eye and playing for high stakes. They dream of stardom, fortune and recognition for all their accomplishments. Surprisingly, perhaps, it appears that many older, more established athletes may use speed, perhaps in an attempt to feel young and prolong their athletic careers. All sorts of sportsmen and women have taken copious amounts of speed to help their performances, leading to doping scandals and the introduction of drug-testing in competitive sports.

During the 1967 Tour de France, which involved a precipitous 18,000m (60,000ft) climb in over 30°C (90°F) heat, the American cyclist Tommy Simpson began to zigzag wildly across the road. Shortly after that, he collapsed on to the road, lapsed into a coma and died. Later, an autopsy was carried out that showed he was heavily drugged with Maxiton – pharmaceutical speed. Shortly thereafter, twenty-three other participants in the race fell sick, with symptoms described by the race doctor as having been caused by "acute amphetamine intoxication". Two rounds later, a newspaper related that *"it was necessary to put one of the contestants in a straight jacket because he suffered an insanity crisis"* after ingesting one hundred Tenedron pills – more pharmaceutical speed.

Speed use became a problem among professional American football players throughout the 1970s. It was studied quite extensively by various professional bodies who identified a phenomenon called the "Sunday Syndrome". This refers to the use of speed to kill pain from injuries, to overcome the sleepiness produced by the pain medication and to get "psyched up" or to heighten their aggressiveness for the game. Dr Arnold Mandell, a locker-room psychoanalyst, observed a range of symptoms including pacing, obscene swearing, vomiting, diarrhoea, and some instances of rage. He claimed that football fans who came to watch the matches were *"buying tickets to see speed-freaks try to kill each other!"* This problem was tackled head-on by the American football authorities and the habit was stamped on ferociously. Speed use was simply not tolerated by the powers-that-be and slowly the habit that had taken over the locker rooms began to recede.

SPEED WRITING

Over the centuries, literature and music have been peppered with allusions to drugs and their effects. It has almost been taken for granted that writers, artists, musicians and other creative types would take drugs to amplify their earthly experiences and feed us mere mortals with the benefit of their insights.

One such creative type, Jack Kerouac, met the poet Allan Ginsberg and the writer William Burroughs when he went to New York in early 1944, after serving as a merchant seaman during the Second World War. Kerouac admired the *"terrible intelligence and style"* of his New York friends. In December 1946, he was introduced to a visitor from Denver, Neal Cassady, who was to become the model for the character Dean Moriarty, in Kerouac's classic novel *On the Road*.

At this time, Kerouac was dividing his time between wild experiments with his friends using different drugs – Benzedrine, morphine, alcohol – and a "straight" life in his parents' household. He took so many drugs with his friends that finally his health began to suffer and he was admitted to hospital after an attack of phlebitis brought on by excessive use of Benzedrine. Kerouac once wrote in his journal about some jazz he had been listening to at that time:

"I like my whiskey wild, I like Saturday night in the shack to be crazy, I like the tenor to be woman-mad, I like things to GO and rock and be flipped, I want to be stoned if I'm going to be stoned at all, I like to be gassed by a back-alley music..."

His attitude toward everything around him was indicative of how much he "liked things to GO". He needed life to be coming at him all guns blazing, all the time. He never tired of looking for and finding that next set of extreme experiences for himself. Speed was a drug that was made for him.

Jack Kerouac's need to be constantly moved, constantly amazed and constantly stimulated was fed by the quantities of speed he was using. He lived on speed when he was trying to write and his most famous work *On the Road* was born out of this kind of speed run. After Kerouac had published his first book, he felt a bit lost. He had been trying for years to write his "road book" with very little success. A fast typist at the best of times, Kerouac hit on the idea of typing non-stop to get the kind of momentum that he wanted in a novel. He was convinced that his verbal flow was being hampered by the need to keep changing the paper when he had finished typing a page. So he taped together ten four-metre (12-foot) long sheets of paper and fed them into his machine in a continuous roll. Visitors to Kerouac's apartment at that time were astounded by the thundering sound of his typewriter, racing non-stop.

His wife, Joan, would arrive home from work and feed him pea soup and coffee. He didn't have the appetite for anything else. He took vast quantities of Benzedrine to stay awake and write. Joan was impressed by the fact that Kerouac sweated so profusely that he went through several T-shirts a day – hanging them up all over the apartment! He had started his book in early April 1951 and by April 27, after much ingestion of speed, the book was finished – 86,000 words typed as a single paragraph nearly forty metres (120 feet) long!

SPEED ON THE ROAD

In this classic Beat novel, *On the Road*, Jack Kerouac defined a whole new American generation. After its publication, William Burroughs described its effect thus: *"After 1957,* On The Road *sold a trillion levis and a million espresso coffee machines, and also sent countless kids on the road."* One passage from the original typescript of his book not only demonstrates his linguistic virtuosity but also shows his appreciation of the search that young America was involved in at that time:

"They rushed down the street together digging everything in the early way they had which has later now become so much sadder and perceptive, but then they danced down the street like dingledodies and I shambled after as usual as I've been doing all my life after people that interest me, because the only people that interest me are the mad ones, the ones who are mad to live, mad to talk, desirous of everything at the same time, the ones that never yearn or say a commonplace thing...but burn, burn, burn like roman candles across the night."

Neal Cassady became a long-time friend and travelling companion of Jack Kerouac. He appears in the book as Dean Moriarty, an amalgam of James Dean, the "rebel without a cause" and the arch Professor Moriarty, the villain of Conan Doyle's Sherlock Holmes stories. Everything about Dean Moriarty, was "mad", "crazy" or "wild". He is probably one of the greatest drivers that literature has ever seen. Kerouac has Moriarty ripping through the country at ninety miles per hour in search of America. But "speed" meant much more to Moriarty than just jamming his foot down on the gas pedal:

"He rubbed his jaw furiously, he swung the car and passed three trucks, he roared into downtown Testament looking in every direction and seeing everything in an arc of 180 degrees around his eyeballs without moving his head. Bang, he found a parking space in no time and we were parked. He leaped out of his car. Furiously, he hustled

into the railway station; we followed sheepishly.... He had become absolutely mad in his movements; he seemed to be doing everything at the same time. It was a shaking of the head, up and down, sideways; jerky, vigorous hands; quick walking; sitting, crossing the legs, uncrossing; getting up, rubbing the hands, rubbing his fly, hitching his pants, looking up and saying 'Am', and sudden slitting of his eyes to see everywhere, and all the time he was grabbing me by the ribs and talking, talking."

One couldn't wish for a more vivid and accurate description of a speed freak. The next year, in 1952, Kerouac holed himself up in Mexico with a large supply of grass and some speed and wrote *Dr Sax*, another rambling exercise in "spontaneous prose". Kerouac went on to write many more autobiographical novels, chronicling the story of his life and his friends. But his sudden death from abdominal haemorrhaging, brought on by alcoholism and drug use, happened in October 1969, before he was able to see his books grow into the legends they came to be.

LIKE FATHER, LIKE SON

In 1970, William S. Burroughs Jnr, son of the author and original beat mentor William Burroughs Snr, published a book called *Speed* with a subjective account of the Lower East Side drug scene. Having been greatly influenced by the Beat generation's insatiable thirst for extreme experiences, he describes his plunge into the world of speed addiction and his own physical and mental deterioration. He portrayed the potential dangers of drug use in vivid and believable terms without the burdensome moralizing that characterized most drug literature of the day. Much more provocative though, was his discussion on his own motives for taking speed.

Burroughs' decision to take drugs was a free choice, a choice that he knew would *"drive him into the ground"*. He rejected the false morality that still cried for man's control of the drug experience and totally surrendered himself to chemistry. His drug use was grounded in a desire to be *"gutted, wired and starved just a bit"* in order to *"see what was up"*. His debilitating three-week speed run in which methamphetamine was injected several times daily in increasingly larger doses, was just one of the ways he tried to prove to himself that he had – *"become a man"*. At the age of 33, he died from liver collapse due to a life full of speed use and alcoholism.

FEAR AND LOATHING

In Aspen, Colorado, where Hunter S. Thompson, the creator and godfather of "Gonzo" journalism, has lived for the past thirty years, opinion about him splits in a disconcerting but instructive way. Some people feel vehemently that he is an out-and-out degenerate and others class him as a national treasure who is a genius and should be cherished.

Thompson is one of those characters who it is safe to call "larger than life". Even if only a small part of his experiences, as related by himself, are true, this would make him a man who spits at proprieties. In his own words, he *"figured that fiction is truer than journalism, anyway"*. A virtual icon, Thompson regularly trashed the prime directives of reporting – accuracy and objectivity – yet nonetheless produced some of the sharpest political and cultural analysis around in the USA. Surrounded by sub-machine guns, fistfuls of colourful pills and the ubiquitous Wild Turkey, Thompson doesn't "go through" his life and career, he careens through them. If Hemingway made heavy drinking respectable, then Thompson opened up the medicine chest.

Thompson's personal story follows the cresting and disintegration of the American Dream. He starts off as an American success story: underprivileged kid from the provinces, a problem boy who never graduated from high school and makes it to the big time as a journalist on his own highly individual terms. He is the quintessential rebel hero, a good guy under a bad rap, thriving on liberal freedoms. His fame starts with a ground-breaking and ecstatically received book about the Hell's Angels and peaks with his classic 1971 reportage on the death of the national dream, *Fear and Loathing in Las Vegas* and his 1972 Presidential election campaign coverage for *Rolling Stone* magazine.

In 1962, Hunter wrote from and about Latin America. He covered elections in Peru and Brazil, mining strikes in Bolivia and the rise of democracy in Ecuador. He published sixteen dispatches, each usually ten or fifteen thousand words long. But it is his letters from that time, reprinted in *Great Shark Hunt*, that show another side to his life out there. He wrote from Peru to his editor complaining that he was losing weight because of dysentery and that he had been bitten by some poison insect, which meant that he couldn't drink any alcohol as it would render useless any medication he took to get better. With no booze to soothe him, Hunter experimented with other substances. It was in South America that he began to use speed regularly.

By the time Hunter got back to the USA and moved to San Francisco, he was already a veteran of many of the drugs coming into vogue. Drugs like Benzedrine, Methedrine, barbiturates and marijuana were already old hat to his bloodstream.

Hunter was happy for people to pop anything they wanted to. With so many people in Haight-Ashbury taking drugs so openly, there was no danger that the police would arrest everyone. But soon Hunter noticed another outlaw lifestyle walking the streets of San Francisco.

The people were unkempt, rode big Harley Davidson motorbikes and liked to travel in packs, proclaiming themselves 'Hell's Angels'. Hunter went on to spend the best part of the next two years following, hanging out with, drinking and taking drugs with the Angels and chronicling their lives and their significance in American culture in a book he simply called *Hell's Angels*.

After falling foul of the Angels, Hunter decided to get as far away as possible and moved to Aspen, Colorado for some peace and quiet and to be able to write. In 1968, Hunter was watching the coverage of the California primaries and saw Bobby Kennedy assassinated. He felt he had witnessed the death of the American dream on television and so, to witness the death "first hand", he went to the Democratic National Convention in Chicago. When he returned to Aspen, he saw the town through newly political eyes. He wrote, *"I went to the Democratic Convention as a journalist and returned a raving beast."* He said the convention had *"permanently altered his brain chemistry"*.

Developers were planning to replace Aspen's quaint old houses and country roads with a four-lane highway and condominiums – to create a tourist haven for the rich – and seemingly didn't care what the locals thought about this. Hunter wasn't having any of this and proposed a new political party: The Freak Power Party. Its aims as reviewed by him in "The Battle for Aspen" in the October 1970 edition of *Rolling Stone* were to: *"create a town where people could live like human beings, instead of slaves to some bogus sense of Progress that is driving us all mad."*

With an artist called Tom Benton, he founded a newspaper, the *Aspen Wallposter*, to overcome some of the negative publicity he was getting in the local paper.

Even drug dealers weren't immune from the *Wallposter's* moralistic editor. He threatened to expose them in print if they "attempt to make any money in Aspen by means of dishonest drug dealing". And he made good his threat by writing about: *"Edson T. Harris III...a seller of extremely rotten mescaline... Probably a combination of nutmeg and rat poison... Avoid any dealing with this person; he sells bad product & refuses to talk about refunds."* He also said in his platform address in 1970 that: *"It will be the general philosophy of the sheriff's office that no drug worth taking should be sold for money."*

Hunter lost that election by only four percentage points. Hunter's journalistic star had risen by now and he was being sent everywhere as the iconoclast who would bash things about a bit. English illustrator Ralph Steadman had become a collaborator on some of Hunter's pieces and was spending a lot of time with him. Their first assignment together was at the Kentucky Derby. Steadman liked working with Hunter but he confessed that Hunter's use of drugs made him nervous.

Hunter said he respected Ralph's point of view: *"I never advocate the use of drugs for everyone, but they have always worked for me."*

In early 1970, Hunter met Oscar Acosta, a Chicano lawyer from Los Angeles and the two of them began to hang out together so that Hunter could write about the Chicano political scene. But Hunter was soon frustrated as he found it difficult to make inroads into this community. He was asked by *Sports Illustrated* to cover the Las Vegas Mint 400 motorcycle race. He tempted Acosta with an all-expenses paid trip to Las Vegas. As Hunter put it, he knew that if he got Acosta to agree, *"we would both go crazy and try to outdo one another. And that's exactly what we did. We fucking stomped the ground in Vegas. We took enough speed to keep Hitler awake in his bunker for fifty days..."*.

Acosta left him in Las Vegas when he couldn't keep up any longer and returned to Los Angeles. By then, Hunter remembered why he had been sent out to Vegas and realized he needed to write. He dug out his usual stash of speed, grass and alcohol, battened down the hatches and went to work. He later wrote: *"It's a rare goddamn trip for a locked-in, rent-paying writer to get a gig that, even in retrospect, was a kinghell, highlife fuckaround from start to finish..."*

The soon-to-be immortal piece began like this:

"We were somewhere around Barstow on the edge of the desert when the drugs began to take hold. I remember saying something like "I feel a bit lightheaded; maybe you should drive..." And suddenly there was a terrible roar all around us and the sky was full of what looked like huge bats, all swooping and screeching and diving around the car, which was going around a hundred miles an hour with the top down to Las Vegas. And a voice was screaming: "Holy Jesus what are these goddamn animals?"

A year after his first trip to Vegas, Hunter delivered the manuscript of *Fear and Loathing in Las Vegas*. It was a running narrative of a weekend in which the journalist Raoul Duke and Dr Gonzo, his *"300 pound Samoan attorney"*, live up to the statement that opens the book: *"He who makes a beast of himself gets rid of the pain of being a man."*

This is the book's description of the drugs that were stashed in their trunk and consumed on the trip: *"two bags of grass, seventy five pellets of mescaline, five sheets of high-powered blotter acid, a salt shaker half full of cocaine, and a whole galaxy of multi-coloured uppers, downers, screamers, laughers...and also a quart of tequila, a quart of rum, a case of Budweiser, a pint of raw ether and two dozen amyls."*

Hunter's erstwhile partner in crime, Ralph Steadman, now gives advice to people who want to engage Hunter S. Thompson to write for them. It's a five-point plan:

1.   *Make certain that everything is paid for in advance.*
2.   *Talk to him every day.*
3.   *Don't let him go home to Aspen if there's work to be done.*
4.   *Fulfil his needs. Alcohol, drugs and room service are necessary to his motivation.*
5.   *Never try to drink as much or do as many drugs as he does. The editor has not been made that can keep up with Hunter's substance habits!*

THE POWER SHOOTERS

When history is being taught, students are rarely offered the insight of knowing that many of the politicians of yore took the very drugs that are demonized today. For example, it wasn't just the armed forces who were using speed during the Second World War. As his own medical records show and many a film newsreel reveals only too clearly, Adolf Hitler was what we would now call a "speed freak", taking both amphetamine tablets, in liberal amounts, and being injected with up to five shots of methamphetamine daily, throughout the duration of the war. The charismatic John F. Kennedy may not have had much in common with the leader of the Third Reich, but there are reports that he did share the Führer's habit of injecting speed.

Even the more restrained Sir Anthony Eden, Conservative Prime Minister of Britain between 1955 and 1957, has said that he was taking Benzedrine every day throughout the military confrontation with Egypt during the Suez Crisis. Speed saw him through the tension of landing British troops in Egypt and the humiliation of having to withdraw them again after widespread international censure. But speed couldn't help him withstand the political backlash that followed and the Prime Minister was forced to resign. These politicians have been lionized and vilified for the power they wielded and the decisions they took while in office. Would Adolf Hitler's followers admire him so much if they knew that enough speed to kill a small horse was coursing through his veins every day? Would it make any difference to an American citizen if he knew that his much-loved and revered President Kennedy was a speed freak?

CONCLUSION

This is not a pro-drugs book. The decision to take or abstain from drugs should be a personal and adult one, as are most other important decisions in life. It isn't the place of anyone to encourage or advocate drug use. That goes as much for licit drugs as illicit drugs.

During the last few decades, society has been able to debate and discuss in public, all manner of thorny and complex issues – pornography, child abuse, paedophilia, television violence and countless others. But the subject of drugs has never been discussed as a public issue without being reduced to a handful of emotionally-potent over simplifications that take serious debate nowhere. It is little wonder that few drugs users will raise their heads above the parapet to speak out on the subject. To admit to taking illicit drugs is to risk losing your job, being denied entry to certain countries, and being ostracized by elements from within your own community and even by close members of your own family. This makes the debate on drugs very one-sided.

Politically, it is even worse. Any politician or party that suggests that the current drug laws and drug policies should be reviewed or changed is immediately slammed as being pro-drug. It is easier and safer these days to bang the law and order drum than address complex social questions with a view to finding solutions. So most politicians either stay silent or join the knee-jerk anti-drugs crusade that crops up with increasing regularity. This ostrich-like, head-in-the-sand attitude towards drugs helps no one – neither those already in trouble, nor more importantly, those waiting in the wings.

Thinking the unthinkable, and arguing for changes in the current drug laws and policies, does not in the least reflect a lack of concern about the undoubted risks that drugs can pose. Rather it reflects an awareness that the present policy is simply not facing up to the predicament the world is in.

INDEX

BIBLIOGRAPHY

Amphetamine and its Analogs – Psychopharmacology, Toxicology and Abuse. Edited by Cho A.K. and Segal D.S. Academic Press, San Diego, 1994.

'The Amphetamines and LSD'. Report by the Advisory Committee on Drug Dependence. London, 1970.

Amphetamine Psychosis. Connell P.H. Oxford University Press, 1958.

A Brief History of Drugs: From the Stone Age to the Stoned Age. Antonio Escohotado. Park Street Press, Vermont, 1996.

The Encyclopaedia of Psychoactive Drugs: Amphetamines: Danger in the Fast Lane. Lukas S.E. Chelsea House Publishers, 1985.

The Encyclopaedia of Psychoactive Substances. Richard Rudgeley. Abacus, 1998.

Fear and Loathing in Las Vegas. Hunter S. Thompson. Granada Publishing, 1971.

Forbidden Drugs. Phillip Robson. Oxford University Press, 1999.

'Ice and Other Methamphetamine Use: An Exploratory Study'. Final Report to the National Institute on Drug Abuse. Morgan P. et al. San Francisco, California, 1994

'Kinship and Community: The 'Ice' Crisis in Hawaii'. Joe Laidler Karen A. and Morgan Patricia. In *'Amphetamine Misuse: International Perspectives on Current Trends'* edited by Hilary Klee. Harwood Academic Publishers, Amsterdam, 1997.

Nightshift. Pete McKenna. S.T. Publishing, Scotland, 1996.

On the Road. Jack Kerouac. Penguin Books, 1955.

A Restrictive Drug Policy: The Swedish Experience. Swedish National Institute of Public Health. Stockholm, 1993.

17th (1970) and 20th (1974) Reports from the Expert Committee on Drug Dependence. World Health Organization (WHO). UN, New York.

Speed. William Burroughs Jnr. Olympia Press, New York, 1970.

The Speed Culture: Amphetamine Use and Abuse in America. Grinspoon L. and Hedblum P. Harvard University Press, 1978

'Stimulants'. A Release guide, 1990

Street Drugs. Andrew Tyler. Coronet Paperbacks, 1986.

'Trends and Patterns of Methamphetamine Smoking in Hawaii'. National Institute on Drug Abuse Research Monograph Series 115. Washington D.C.– Supt of Documents, US Govt Printing Office, 1991.

United Nations Report: Convention on Psychotropic Substances, 1971. UN, New York, 1977

United Nations Report of the International Narcotics Control Board. UN New York, 1993.

Waiting for the Man. Harry Shapiro. Helter Skelter Publishing, 1999.